GRADES 3-4

...the Super Source™

Pat

Cuisenaire Company of America, Inc.
White Plains, NY

Cuisenaire extends its warmest thanks to the many teachers and students across the country who helped ensure the success of the Super Source™ series by participating in the outlining, writing, and field testing of the materials.

Project Director: Judith Adams
Managing Editor: Doris Hirschhorn
Editorial Team: Patricia Kijak Anderson, Linda Dodge, John Nelson, Deborah J. Slade, Harriet Slonim
Field Test Coordinator: Laurie Verdeschi

Design Manager: Phyllis Aycock
Text Design: Amy Berger, Tracey Munz
Line Art and Production: Joan Lee, Fiona Santoianni
Cover Design: Michael Muldoon
Illustrations: Rebecca Thornburgh

...the Super Source™

Table of Contents

INTRODUCTION
  USING *THE SUPER SOURCE*™ 4
  EXPLORING PATTERN BLOCKS 9

STRANDS AND TOPICS 12

OVERVIEW OF THE LESSONS 16

LESSONS
  Blue and Green Triangles 18
  Boats and Boxes 22
  Building Congruent Hexagons 26
  Congruent Shapes 30
  Hexiamonds 34
  Make My Design 38
  Only Two Blocks 42
  Recover the Symmetry 46
  Riddle Makers 50
  Size Them Up! 54
  Spiney and Other Creatures 58
  The Last Block 62
  Tiling 66
  Trapezoids 1–16 70
  What's My Shape Worth? 74
  What's Next? 78
  What's the Perimeter? 82
  Wipe Out! 86

BLACKLINE MASTERS
  Pattern Block Triangle Paper 90
  Pattern Block Shapes 91
  Boats and Boxes Spinner 92
  The Last Block Game Board 93
  Pattern Block Writing Paper 94
  Pattern Block Tracing and Writing Paper 95

Using the Super Source™

The Super Source™ is a series of books, each of which contains a collection of activities to use with a specific math manipulative. Driving **the Super Source**™ is Cuisenaire's conviction that children construct their own understandings through rich, hands-on mathematical experiences. Although the activities in each book are written for a specific grade range, they all connect to the core of mathematics learning that is important to every K-6 child. Thus, the material in many activities can easily be refocused for children at other grade levels. Because the activities are not arranged sequentially, children can work on any activity at any time.

The lessons in **the Super Source**™ all follow a basic structure consistent with the vision of mathematics teaching described in the *Curriculum and Evaluation Standards for School Mathematics* published by the National Council of Teachers of Mathematics.

All of the activities in this series involve Problem Solving, Communication, Reasoning, and Mathematical Connections—the first four NCTM Standards. Each activity also focuses on one or more of the following curriculum strands: Number, Geometry, Measurement, Patterns/Functions, Probability/Statistics, Logic.

HOW LESSONS ARE ORGANIZED

At the beginning of each lesson, you will find, to the right of the title, both the major curriculum strands to which the lesson relates and the particular topics that children will work with. Each lesson has three main sections. The first, GETTING READY, offers an *Overview*, which states what children will be doing, and why, and provides a list of "What You'll Need." Specific numbers of Pattern Blocks are suggested on this list but can be adjusted as the needs of your specific situation dictate. Before an activity, blocks can be counted out and placed in containers or self-sealing plastic bags for easy distribution. When crayons are called for, it is understood that their colors are those that match the Pattern Blocks and that markers may be used in place of crayons. Blackline masters that are provided for your convenience at the back of the book are also referenced on this materials list. Paper, pencils, scissors, tape, and materials for making charts, which may be necessary in certain activities, are usually not.

Although overhead Pattern Blocks are always listed in "What You'll Need" as optional, these materials are highly effective when you want to demonstrate the use of Pattern Blocks. As you move blocks on the screen, children can work with the same materials at their seats. If overhead Pattern Blocks are not available, you may want to make and use transparencies of the Pattern Block shapes (see page 91). Children can also use the overhead Pattern Blocks and/or a transparency of the triangle paper to present their work to other members of their group or to the class.

The second section, THE ACTIVITY, first presents a possible scenario for *Introducing* the children to the activity. The aim of this brief introduction is to help you give children the tools they will need to investigate independently. However, care has been taken to avoid undercutting the activity itself. Since these investigations are designed to enable children to increase their own mathematical power, the idea is to set the stage but not steal the show! The heart of the lesson, *On Their Own*, is found in a box at the top of the second page of each lesson. Here, rich problems stimulate many different problem-solving approaches and lead to a variety of solutions. These hands-on explorations have the potential for bringing children to new mathematical ideas and deepening skills.

On Their Own is intended as a stand-alone activity for children to explore with a partner or in a small group. Be sure to make the needed directions clearly visible. You may want to write them on the chalkboard or on an overhead or present them either on reusable cards or paper. For children who may have difficulty reading the directions, you can read them aloud or make sure that at least one "reader" is in each group.

The last part of this second section, *The Bigger Picture*, gives suggestions for how children can share their work and their thinking and make mathematical connections. Class charts and children's recorded work provide a springboard for discussion. Under "Thinking and Sharing," there are several prompts that you can use to promote discussion. Children will not be able to respond to these prompts with one-word answers. Instead, the prompts encourage children to describe what they notice, tell how they found their results, and give the reasoning behind their answers. Thus children learn to verify their own results rather than relying on the teacher to determine if an answer is "right" or "wrong." Though the class discussion might immediately follow the investigation, it is important not to cut the activity short by having a class discussion too soon.

The Bigger Picture often includes a suggestion for a "Writing" (or drawing) assignment. This is meant to help children process what they have just been doing. You might want to use these ideas as a focus for daily or weekly entries in a math journal that each child keeps.

① Yes, because perimeter it depends on the number of side's it's showing.

② The smallest perimeters was tightly paake and the largest would be spread out.

③ It is possible because some blocks fit nicely together.

From: *What's the Perimeter?*

No I have not found all the possibility's, But I have done as much as I can.

I took 6 triangles and just put them together.

They are congruent.

Yes I did. I sorted them by the number of sides

From: *Hexiamonds*

The Bigger Picture always ends with ideas for "Extending the Activity." Extensions take the essence of the main activity and either alter or extend its parameters. These activities are well used with a class that becomes deeply involved in the primary activity or for children who finish before the others. In any case, it is probably a good idea to expose the entire class to the possibility of, and the results from, such extensions.

The third and final section of the lesson is TEACHER TALK. Here, in *Where's the Mathematics?*, you can gain insight into the underlying mathematics of the activity and discover some of the strategies children are apt to use as they work. Solutions are also given—when such are necessary and/or helpful. Because *Where's the Mathematics?* provides a view of what may happen in the lesson as well as the underlying mathematical potential that may grow out of it, this may be the section that you want to read before presenting the activity to children.

USING THE ACTIVITIES

The Super Source™ has been designed to fit into the variety of classroom environments in which it will be used. These range from a completely manipulative-based classroom to one in which manipulatives are just beginning to play a part. You may choose to use some activities in **the Super Source**™ in the way set forth in each lesson (introducing an activity to the whole class, then breaking the class up into groups that all work on the same task, and so forth). You will then be able to circulate among the groups as they work to observe and perhaps comment on each child's work. This approach requires a full classroom set of materials but allows you to concentrate on the variety of ways that children respond to a given activity.

Alternatively, you may wish to make two or three related activities available to different groups of children at the same time. You may even wish to use different manipulatives to explore the same mathematical concept. (Geoboards and Tangrams, for example, can be used to teach some of the same geometric principles as Pattern Blocks.) This approach does not require full classroom sets of a particular manipulative. It also permits greater adaptation of materials to individual children's needs and/or preferences.

If children are comfortable working independently, you might want to set up a "menu"— that is, set out a number of related activities from which children can choose. Children should be encouraged to write about their experiences with these independent activities.

However you choose to use **the Super Source**™ activities, it would be wise to allow time for several groups or the entire class to share their experiences. The dynamics of this type of interaction, where children share not only solutions and strategies but also feelings and intuitions, is the basis of continued mathematical growth. It allows children who are beginning to form a mathematical structure to clarify it and those who have mastered just isolated concepts to begin to see how these concepts might fit together.

Again, both the individual teaching style and combined learning styles of the children should dictate the specific method of utilizing **the Super Source**™ lessons. At first sight, some activities may appear too difficult for some of your children, and you may find yourself tempted to actually "teach" by modeling exactly how an activity can lead to a particular learning outcome. If you do this, you rob children of the chance to try the activity in whatever way they can. As long as children have a way to begin an investigation, give them time and opportunity to see it through. Instead of making assumptions about what children will or won't do, watch and listen. The excitement and challenge of the activity—as well as the chance to work cooperatively—may bring out abilities in children that will surprise you.

If you are convinced, however, that an activity does not suit your students, adjust it, by all means. You may want to change the language, either by simplifying it or by referring to specific vocabulary that you and your children already use and are comfortable with. On the other hand, if you suspect that an activity isn't challenging enough, you may want to read through the activity extensions for a variation that you can give children instead.

RECORDING

Although the direct process of working with Pattern Blocks is a valuable one, it is afterward, when children look at, compare, share, and think about their constructions, that an activity yields its greatest rewards. However, because Pattern Block designs can't always be left intact for very long, children need an effective way to record their work. To this end, at the back of this book recording paper is provided for reproduction. The "What You'll Need" listing at the beginning of each lesson often specifies the kind of recording paper to use. For example, in an activity where children are working with only the yellow, red, blue, and green Pattern Blocks, they can duplicate their work or trace the Pattern Block pieces on the Pattern Block triangle paper found on page 90.

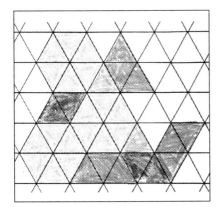

From: *What's My Shape Worth?*

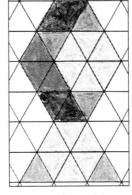

From: *What's My Shape Worth?*

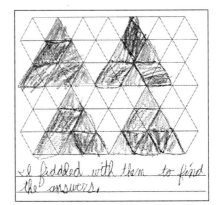

From: *Blue and Green Triangles*

When they also work with the orange and/or tan Pattern Blocks, children need a plain piece of recording paper, since these Pattern Block pieces don't fit neatly onto the triangle paper.

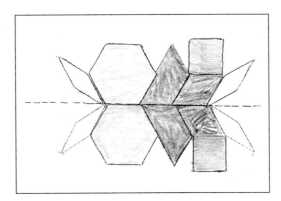

From: *Recover the Symmetry*

In this latter case, the children will have to find a way to transfer their Pattern Block designs. They might choose to trace each Pattern Block piece in the design onto the plain paper or to use a Pattern Block template to reproduce each piece in the design. Templates of the exact size and shape of the Pattern Blocks can be bought or made from plastic coffee-can lids.

When young children explore Pattern Blocks, they are likely to use up every available block in making a huge pattern. This makes the pattern daunting to copy. Such patterns may be recorded using cutouts of the Pattern Block shapes (see page 91). Children can color the shapes and paste them in place on white paper.

Another interesting way to "freeze" a Pattern Block design is to create it using a software piece, such as *Shape Up!*, and then get a printout. Children can use a classroom or resource-room computer if it is available or, where possible, extend the activity into a home assignment by utilizing their home computers.

Recording involves more than copying the designs. Writing, drawing, and making charts and tables are also ways to record. By creating a table of data gathered in the course of their investigations, children are able to draw conclusions and look for patterns. When children write or draw, either in their group or later by themselves, they are clarifying their understanding of their recent mathematical experience.

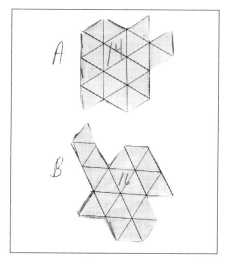

From: *What's the Perimeter?*

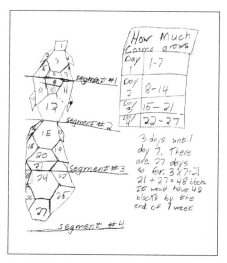

From: *Spiney and Other Creatures*

1.	Three of the blue blocks makes up the first shape
2.	The blue block needs two of these to make one
3.	a blue and green block makes up one of these

From: *Riddle Makers*

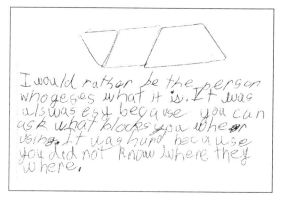

I would rather be the person who geses what it is. It was als was esy because you can ask what blocks you whe you using. It was hurd because you did not know where they where.

From: *Make My Design*

With a roomful of children busily engaged in their investigations, it is not easy for a teacher to keep track of how individual children are working. Having tangible material to gather and examine when the time is right will help you to keep in close touch with each child's learning.

Exploring Pattern Blocks

A set of Pattern Blocks consists of blocks in six geometric, color-coded shapes, referred to as: green triangles, orange squares, blue parallelograms, tan rhombuses, red trapezoids, and yellow hexagons. The relationships among the side measures and among the angle measures make it very easy to fit the blocks together to make tiling patterns which completely cover a flat surface. The blocks are designed so that all the sides of the shapes are 1 inch except the longer side of the trapezoid, which is 2 inches, or twice as long as the other sides. Except for the tan rhombus, which has two angles which that measure 150°, all of the shapes have angles whose measures are factors of 360—120°, 90°, 60°, and 30°. Yet even these 150° angles relate to the other angles, since 150° is the sum of 90° and 60°.

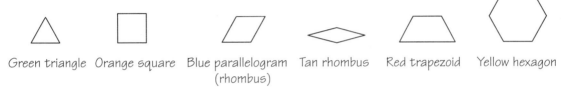

| Green triangle | Orange square | Blue parallelogram (rhombus) | Tan rhombus | Red trapezoid | Yellow hexagon |

These features of the Pattern Blocks encourage investigation of relationships among the shapes. One special aspect of the shapes is that the yellow block can be covered exactly by putting together two red blocks, or three blue blocks, or six green blocks. This is a natural lead-in to the consideration of how fractional parts relate to a whole—the yellow block. Thus, when children work only with the yellow, red, blue, and green blocks, and the yellow block is chosen as the unit, then a red block represents 1/2, a blue block represents 1/3, and a green block represents 1/6. Within this small world of fractions, children can develop hands-on familiarity and intuition about comparing fractions, finding equivalent fractions, changing improper fractions to mixed numbers, and modeling addition, subtraction, division, and multiplication of fractions.

Pattern Blocks provide a visual image which is essential for real understanding of fraction algorithms. Many children learn to do examples such as "3 $\frac{1}{2}$ = ?/2," "1/2 x 1/3 = ?" or "4 ÷ 1/3 = ?" at a purely symbolic level so that if they forget the procedure, they are at a total loss. Yet children who have had many presymbolic experiences solving problems like "Find how many red blocks fit over three yellows and a red," "Find half of the blue block," or "Find how many blue blocks cover four yellow blocks" will have a solid intuitive foundation on which to build these skills and to fall back on if memory fails them.

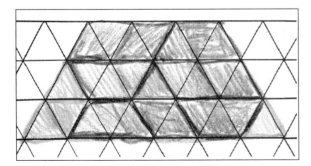

From: *Trapezoids 1–16*

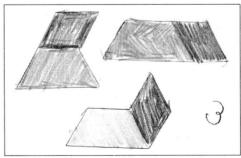

From: *Only Two Blocks*

Children do need ample time to experiment freely with Pattern Blocks, however, before they begin more serious investigations. Most children can begin without additional direction, but some may need suggestions. Asking children to find the different shapes, sizes, and colors of Pattern Blocks, or asking them to cover their desktops with the blocks or to find which blocks can be used to build straight roads, might be good for "starters."

WORKING WITH PATTERN BLOCKS

As children begin to work with Pattern Blocks, they use them primarily to explore spatial relations. Young children have an initial tendency to work with others and to copy one another's designs. Yet even duplicating another's pattern with blocks can expand a child's experience, develop ability to recognize similarities and differences, and provide a context for developing language related to geometric ideas. Throughout their investigations, children should be encouraged to talk about their constructions. Expressing their thoughts out loud helps children to clarify and extend their thinking.

Pattern Blocks help children to explore many mathematical topics, including congruence, similarity, symmetry, area, perimeter, patterns, functions, fractions, and graphing. The following are just a few of the possibilities:

When playing "exchange games" with the various sized blocks, children can develop an understanding of relationships between objects with different values, such as coins or place-value models.

When trying to identify which blocks can be put together to make another shape, children can begin to build a base for the concept of fractional pieces.

When the blocks are used to completely fill in an outline, the concept of area is developed. If children explore measuring the same area using different blocks as units they can develop understandings about the relationship of the size of the unit and the measure of the area.

When investigating the perimeter of shapes made with Pattern Blocks, children can discover that shapes with the same area can have different perimeters and that shapes with the same perimeter can have different areas.

When using Pattern Blocks to cover a flat surface, children can discover that some combinations of corners, or angles, fit together or can be arranged around a point. Knowing that a full circle measures 360° enables children to find the various angle measurements.

When finding how many blocks of the same color it takes to make a larger shape similar to the original block (which can be done with all but the yellow hexagon), children can discover the square number pattern—1, 4, 9, 16, ...

Margo   name of creatrae
Mon. Tue. Wed. Thurs. Fri. Sat. Sun.
3+4+3+3+3+3+3+3+3+3+3 = 34

From: *Spiney and Other Creatures*

ASSESSING CHILDREN'S UNDERSTANDING

The use of Pattern Blocks provides a perfect opportunity for authentic assessment. Watching children work with the blocks gives you a sense of how they approach a mathematical problem. Their thinking can be "seen" through their positioning of the Pattern Blocks. When a class breaks up into small working groups, you are able to circulate, listen, and raise questions, all the while focusing on how individuals are thinking.

The challenges that children encounter when working with Pattern Blocks often elicit unexpected abilities from children whose performance in more symbolic, number-oriented tasks may be weak. On the other hand, some children with good memories for numerical relationships have difficulty with spatial challenges and can more readily learn from freely exploring with Pattern Blocks. Thus, by observing children's free exploration, you can get a sense of individual styles and intellectual strengths.

Having children describe their creations and share their strategies and thinking with the whole class gives you another opportunity for observational assessment. Furthermore, you may want to gather children's recorded work or invite them to choose pieces to add to their math portfolios.

From: *What's My Shape Worth?*

From: *What's My Shape Worth?*

Models of teachers assessing children's understanding can be found in Cuisenaire's series of videotapes listed below.

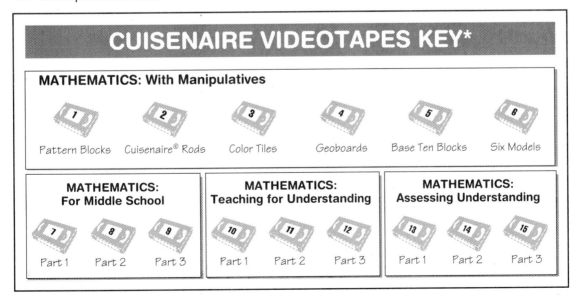

*See *Overview of the Lessons*, pages 16–17, for specific lesson/video correlation.

STRANDS

Connect *the Super Source*™ to NCTM Standards.

	PROBLEM SOLVING	COMMUNICATION	REASONING	CONNECTIONS	Geometry	Logic	Measurement	Number	Patterns/Functions	Probability/Statistics
BLUE AND GREEN TRIANGLES	◆	◆	◆	◆	◆					
BOATS AND BOXES	◆	◆	◆	◆			◆	◆	◆	
BUILDING CONGRUENT HEXAGONS	◆	◆	◆	◆	◆					
CONGRUENT SHAPES	◆	◆		◆	◆					
HEXIAMONDS	◆	◆	◆	◆	◆	◆				
MAKE MY DESIGN	◆	◆	◆	◆	◆	◆				
ONLY TWO BLOCKS	◆	◆	◆	◆						
RECOVER THE SYMMETRY	◆		◆	◆	◆					
RIDDLE MAKERS	◆	◆	◆	◆	◆	◆				
SIZE THEM UP!	◆	◆	◆	◆	◆		◆			
SPINEY & OTHER CREATURES	◆	◆	◆	◆					◆	
THE LAST BLOCK	◆	◆	◆	◆		◆				
TILING	◆	◆	◆	◆						
TRAPEZOIDS 1–16	◆		◆	◆	◆				◆	
WHAT'S MY SHAPE WORTH?	◆	◆	◆	◆		◆		◆		
WHAT'S NEXT?	◆	◆	◆	◆	◆				◆	
WHAT'S THE PERIMETER?	◆	◆	◆	◆	◆		◆			
WIPE OUT!	◆	◆	◆	◆	◆			◆		◆

TOPICS

Correlate
the Super Source™
to your curriculum.

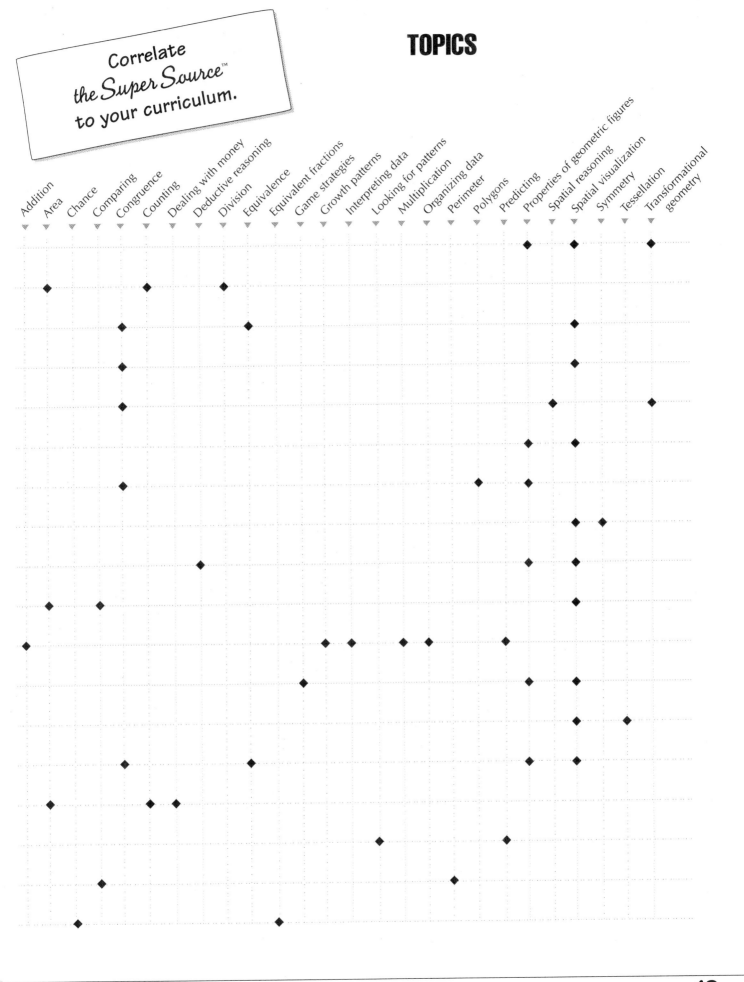

Classroom-tested activities contained in these *Super Source*™ Pattern Blocks books focus on the math strands in the charts below.

...*the Super Source*™ **Pattern Blocks, Grades K-2**

Geometry	Logic	Measurement
Number	Patterns/Functions	Probability/Statistics

...*the Super Source*™ **Pattern Blocks, Grades 5-6**

Geometry	Logic	Measurement
Number	Patterns/Functions	Probability/Statistics

Classroom-tested activities contained in these *Super Source™* books focus on the math strands as indicated in these charts.

the Super Source™ Snap™ Cubes, Grades 3-4

Geometry	Logic	Measurement
Number	**Patterns/Functions**	**Probability/Statistics**

the Super Source™ Cuisenaire® Rods, Grades 3-4

Geometry	Logic	Measurement
Number	**Patterns/Functions**	

the Super Source™ Geoboards, Grades 3-4

Geometry	Logic	Measurement
Number	**Patterns/Functions**	

the Super Source™ Color Tiles, Grades 3-4

Geometry	Logic	Measurement
Number	**Patterns/Functions**	**Probability/Statistics**

the Super Source™ Tangrams, Grades 3-4

Geometry	Logic	Measurement
Number	**Patterns/Functions**	**Probability/Statistics**

Overview of the Lessons

BLUE AND GREEN TRIANGLES 18

Properties of geometric figures, Spatial visualization, Transformational geometry

Children investigate the different ways they can arrange three blue and three green Pattern Blocks to make triangles.

BOATS AND BOXES 22

Division, Counting, Area

In this game for two players, children work together using Pattern Blocks to model a problem involving the number of "boats" needed to carry a given number of "boxes."

 BUILDING CONGRUENT HEXAGONS 26

Spatial visualization, Congruence, Equivalence

Children search to find all possible combinations of Pattern Blocks that can be used to build shapes congruent to the yellow hexagon.

CONGRUENT SHAPES 30

Spatial visualization, Congruence

Children create a shape using four Pattern Blocks and then use other combinations or arrangements of blocks to build shapes that are congruent to the original.

HEXIAMONDS 34

Spatial reasoning, Congruence, Transformational geometry

Children search to find all the different arrangements that can be made using six green Pattern Block triangles.

MAKE MY DESIGN 38

Spatial visualization, Properties of geometric figures

Children create Pattern Block designs and take turns describing the designs so that their partner can recreate them without seeing them.

ONLY TWO BLOCKS 42

Properties of geometric figures, Congruence, Polygons

Children try to create as many different shapes as possible using combinations of two different Pattern Blocks. They then record and sort the shapes they have made.

RECOVER THE SYMMETRY 46

Symmetry, Spatial visualization

In this game for two players, children create symmetrical designs with Pattern Blocks, disturb the symmetry, and then challenge a partner to restore symmetry to their design.

RIDDLE MAKERS 50

Properties of geometric figures, Spatial visualization, Deductive reasoning

Children create riddles that provide clues about Pattern Blocks that they have hidden in a paper bag. They then try to solve each other's riddles.

See video key, page 11.

Pattern Blocks, Grades 3-4

SIZE THEM UP! 54

Area, Comparing, Spatial visualization

Children make shapes with Pattern Blocks, trace the outlines of their shapes, and arrange the outlines in what they perceive to be size order. They then look for different ways to check that they have ordered their shapes correctly.

SPINEY AND OTHER CREATURES 58

Organizing data, Interpreting data, Addition, Multiplication, Growth patterns, Predicting with patterns

Children build Pattern Block creatures that grow in predictable ways. They then try to predict what their creatures will look like and how many blocks it will take to build them after seven stages of growth.

THE LAST BLOCK. 62

Spatial visualization, Properties of geometric figures, Game strategies

In this game for two or four players, children take turns placing Pattern Blocks on a hexagonal game board. The winner is the player who places the last block on the board.

TILING 66

Spatial visualization, Tessellation

Children investigate which two-color combinations of Pattern Blocks can be used to tile a surface.

TRAPEZOIDS 1–16 70

Properties of geometric figures, Spatial visualization, Congruence, Equivalence

Children build trapezoids using specified numbers of Pattern Blocks.

WHAT'S MY SHAPE WORTH? 74

Counting, Dealing with money, Area

Children create Pattern Block designs and determine the "monetary value" of their designs based on a value assigned to one of the shapes.

WHAT'S NEXT? 78

Looking for patterns, Predicting

Children create, record, and predict repeating patterns using Pattern Blocks. They then relate their patterns to number patterns by using a hundreds chart.

WHAT'S THE PERIMETER? 82

Perimeter, Comparing geometric shapes

Children investigate the different perimeters of shapes that can be made using one set of six Pattern Blocks.

WIPE OUT! 86

Equivalent fractions, Chance

In this game for two players, children use Pattern Blocks to represent fractional parts of the yellow hexagon.

See video key, page 11.

BLUE AND GREEN TRIANGLES

• Properties of geometric figures
• Spatial visualization
• Transformational geometry

Getting Ready

What You'll Need

Pattern Blocks, 3 blue and 3 green per child

Crayons

Pattern Block triangle paper, page 90

Overhead Pattern Blocks (optional)

Overview

Children investigate the different ways they can arrange three blue and three green Pattern Blocks to make triangles. In this activity, children have the opportunity to:

◆ use spatial skills to fit shapes together to make a larger shape

◆ use flips and turns to check for uniqueness of solutions

◆ consider ways to determine if all solutions have been found

The Activity

Introducing

◆ Ask children to use two green triangles and one blue rhombus to make a triangle.

◆ Call on volunteers to display the triangles they made.

◆ Volunteers can either recreate their triangles on the overhead or trace, color, and cut them out.

◆ Ask children how these triangles are different and how they are alike.

◆ Establish that they are alike because they all can be turned to look the same.

©1996 Cuisenaire Company of America, Inc.

On Their Own

> How many different ways can you arrange 3 green triangles and 3 blue parallelograms to form a triangle?
>
> - Use all 6 Pattern Blocks to make triangles in as many different ways as you can.
>
> - Use blue and green crayons to record each different solution on triangle paper.
>
> - Check to see whether all your solutions are different. If any triangle can be flipped or turned to look like another, don't count it as a new solution.

The Bigger Picture

Thinking and Sharing

Invite volunteers to post their solutions. Have children check for and remove any duplicates.

Use prompts such as these to promote class discussion:

- How did you go about finding your solutions?

- At some point, did you discover that you had duplicates? How did you know?

- Do you think you have found all the solutions? If you do, what makes you think so?

- Did the sizes and shapes of the Pattern Blocks help you in any way?

Extending the Activity

1. Have children explore the different ways they can arrange four green and six blue Pattern Blocks to make triangles. Then have them repeat the investigation using three green blocks and two red blocks.

2. Have children investigate the different ways they can arrange four green and three blue blocks to make hexagons.

Where's the Mathematics?

There are five unique arrangements for building a triangle using three green triangles and three blue parallelograms.

Children may search for solutions in a variety of ways. Some children may randomly build as many triangles as they can, without giving much thought to developing a systematic approach. Other children might start with one triangle and then rearrange two or more blocks at a time until they think that they have exhausted all the possibilities for placement. For example, beginning with triangle A below, a child might interchange the parallelogram and triangle at the upper left and wind up with triangle B. By interchanging the parallelogram and triangle at the lower right of triangle B, they would get triangle C.

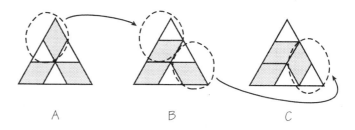

Children who realize that two green triangles can be put together to form a shape that is congruent to the blue parallelogram may try to use this equivalence to create new solutions from existing ones. They find, however, that such a substitution (one blue block for two green blocks, or two green blocks for one blue block) does not work. In fact, in order for the six shapes to form a triangle, no green triangles may share a side.

No matter what strategies children use, they are likely to have made some arrangements that are duplicates of one another. Since all the triangle arrangements have exactly the same size and shape, identifying duplicates may be difficult for some children. Many will focus on the placement of the green triangles within the arrangements to help them find solutions that may be duplicates. Although some children may be able to compare shapes through visualization alone, other children may need to physically maneuver their actual triangles to see if arrangements are the same or different. Some children may record all of the solutions they find, cut them apart, and manipulate the recordings to see whether solutions are flips or turns of one another.

Children may be surprised to find that there are only five different arrangements that can be made. However, in trying to make different arrangements beyond these five, they may make some observations that may help them feel assured that no other solutions exist. For example, if children discover that the green triangles may not share a side in the arrangement, they may experiment with all the different possible combinations of positions for the three green triangles, only to find that there are only five that are not flips or turns of one another.

BOATS AND BOXES

• Division
• Counting
• Area

Getting Ready

What You'll Need

Pattern Blocks, 15 yellow and 24 each of red, blue, and green per pair

Boats and Boxes spinners, 1 per pair, page 92

Overhead Pattern Blocks (optional)

Overview

In this game for two players, children work together using Pattern Blocks to model a problem involving the number of "boats" needed to carry a given number of "boxes." In this activity, children have the opportunity to:

♦ informally model division situations

♦ recognize the relationship between multiplication and repeated addition

♦ explore patterns

The Activity

Make sure children understand that blocks should cover the hexagon in a single layer and that stacking is not allowed.

Introducing

♦ Display a yellow hexagon.

♦ Ask children to find the number of blue blocks that can fit on the yellow block. Then have them do the same for green blocks and for red blocks.

On Their Own

Play *Boats and Boxes!*

Here are the rules:

1. This is a game for 2 players. Players pretend that the yellow blocks are boats and the other blocks are boxes. The object is to find the number of boats needed to take boxes across a lake.

2. Players spin the spinner once. They take that number of red blocks.

3. Players figure out how many boats they will need to take their red boxes across the lake. They record their results.

4. Then players figure out how many boats they would need for the same number of blue boxes, then for the same number of green boxes. They record their results.

- Play *Boats and Boxes* at least 3 times. If you spin a number you have already spun, spin a new number.

- Be ready to talk about patterns you notice.

The Bigger Picture

Thinking and Sharing

Invite children to discuss their observations about the game. Have them help you fill in a class chart like this:

How many boxes must go?	What's the color of the box?	How many boxes fit on a boat?	How many boats do we need?	How many boats are full?	How many boxes are in the last boat?

Use prompts like these to promote class discussion:

- What did you find out about filling boats with different numbers and sizes of boxes?

- Which kind of boxes needed the most boats? Why?

- Which kind of boxes needed the fewest boats? Why?

- Were you always able to fill all your boats? If not, how did you arrange your boxes? Was there empty space in just one boat or in more than one boat?

- Did anyone find a different way to place a particular number of boxes on the boats? Describe what you did.

- Did you notice any patterns? If so, describe them.

Writing

Have children choose a number greater than 24 and explain how they might figure out the number of boats needed to carry this number of green boxes across a lake.

Teacher Talk

Where's the Mathematics?

This activity provides an opportunity for an informal exploration of the concepts that underlie division and multiplication. In modeling the problem, children divide quantities of boxes (dividend) by the number of boxes known to fit on a boat (divisor) to find the number of boats that will be filled (quotient) and the number of boxes that will be on a last, unfilled boat (remainder). Similarly, by adding boat after boat with the same number of boxes, children are also modeling multiplication. However, although this work provides a concrete representation of multiplication and division, it is not important that children use this vocabulary in discussing the activity.

Children are apt to solve this problem in different ways. Some children may methodically fill each boat, and then place any leftover boxes on the last boat. For example:

Uncovered
(yellow)

15 green boxes
3 boats
The boats carry 6 boxes, 6 boxes, and 3 boxes.

Other children may attempt to distribute the boxes evenly among the boats once they see that the last boat will not be full.

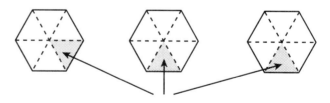

Uncovered (yellow)

15 green boxes
3 boats
5 boxes on each boat

Extending the Activity

1. Provide groups with mixed cargo: collections of green, blue, and red shapes. Ask children to find how many yellow boats they will need to take the cargo across the lake. Have children draw their solutions.

2. Have children combine Pattern Blocks to create their own boats. Have them then trace the outline of their boat and find how many of these boats will be needed to carry various numbers and sizes of boxes across the lake.

Regardless of how they choose to arrange their boxes, children have the opportunity to make a number of observations. They are likely to recognize that the greater the number of boxes that can fit on each boat, the fewer the number of boats that are needed. Some children may describe this in terms of the size of the boxes, noting that fewer boats are needed when the boxes themselves are smaller. This observation may help children to see the relationship between the areas of the blocks that are the different-sized boxes and the number of boats needed.

Some relationships may become more obvious to children when the class data is assembled. Children may notice that when the different-sized boxes can each be distributed evenly among the boats, with each boat full (as is the case when either 12, 18, or 24 is spun), the number of boats needed for blue boxes is twice the number needed for green boxes, and the number of boats needed for red boxes is three times the number needed for green boxes. Children may or may not be able to explain the reason for this, although some may realize that one blue Pattern Block is equivalent to two green and that one red Pattern Block is equivalent to three green.

Children may also recognize that when the number of boxes is a multiple of the number of boxes that can fit on one boat, no boats are needed beyond those that can be filled. They may further notice that when the number spun is not a multiple of the number of boxes that can fit on one boat, the number of "extra" boxes that require an additional boat is the difference between the number spun and a multiple of the number of boxes that can fit on one boat. This observation may lead some to see how the data relates to the dividend, divisor, quotient, and remainder in a division problem.

Children may have different ways of interpreting their solutions. For example, in the problem pictured on the previous page, children may describe three boats making a single trip or one boat making three trips. In cases where the last boat is close to being empty, some children may even decide to leave the leftover boxes behind, reasoning that it is not practical to use a final boat or make a final trip for such a small cargo. With all solutions, encourage children to describe the consequences of their solution—what they are doing with the boats and what happens to the boxes—in addition to giving the numbers involved. Such discussion reinforces the links between problems, models, and the real-world situations they represent and helps children understand the implications of their solutions.

BUILDING CONGRUENT HEXAGONS

- Spatial visualization
- Congruence
- Equivalence

Getting Ready

What You'll Need

Pattern Blocks, about 50 per pair

Pattern Block triangle paper, page 90

Crayons

Overhead Pattern Blocks (optional)

Overview

Children search to find all possible combinations of Pattern Blocks that can be used to build shapes congruent to the yellow hexagon. In this activity, children have the opportunity to:

- reinforce understanding of congruency and equivalence
- assess the uniqueness of solutions
- develop spatial reasoning skills

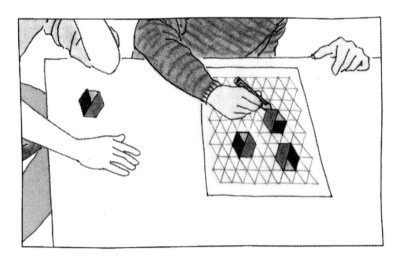

The Activity

Some children may think they have additional solutions. Show them that other solutions are simply different arrangements of the blue-green combination.

Introducing

- Have children put down a red trapezoid. Ask them to use other Pattern Blocks to form a shape that could cover the red trapezoid exactly.

- Invite a volunteer to show that his or her arrangement of blocks fits exactly over the red trapezoid. Explain that when two shapes have exactly the same size and shape, they are *congruent*.

- Ask if anyone used a different combination of blocks. Display this second combination. Establish that there are only two different combinations that make a shape congruent to the red trapezoid.

On Their Own

How many different combinations of Pattern Blocks can you use to make shapes that are congruent to the yellow hexagon?

- With a partner, use Pattern Blocks to make shapes that are the same size and shape as the yellow hexagon.

- Each shape should use a different combination of blocks. If 2 shapes use only a different arrangement of the same blocks, the second shape should not count as a new combination.

- Record your shapes on triangle paper. Then color them in.

- Be ready to explain how you know you have found all the solutions.

The Bigger Picture

Thinking and Sharing

Invite volunteers to post some of their solutions. Continue until children are satisfied that all possible combinations are displayed.

Use prompts such as these to promote class discussion:

- What were some of your strategies for finding shapes?

- How did you make sure your solutions were all different?

- What helped you decide that you had found all the possible combinations?

- Why didn't you use the orange square and the tan parallelogram?

Extending the Activity

1. Have children repeat the activity, but change the rules so that solutions include different arrangements of the same blocks.

2. Direct children to find the different combinations of Pattern Blocks that can be used to build equilateral triangles whose sides are 3 units long, where 1 unit is the length of a side of a green triangle.

Where's the Mathematics?

There are seven different solutions for this activity.

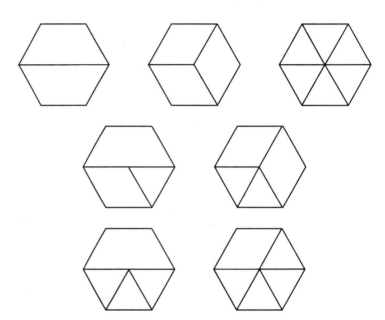

Many children may start by trying to make hexagons using several blocks of the same shape. In their search for additional solutions, children move naturally into the realm of equivalency and substitution, two important concepts in mathematics. Some children may change their same-block solutions by removing one block at a time, then testing whether the empty space can be filled by one or more of another kind of block. For example, a child might take one green triangle away from a hexagon made from six green triangles, then one more green triangle away from the remaining five, to discover that the empty space can be filled by one blue parallelogram.

Some children may use strategies based on equivalences among the Pattern Block shapes. In the following sequence of hexagons, one of the red trapezoids in hexagon A is replaced by a blue parallelogram and a green triangle to form hexagon B. The blue parallelogram in hexagon B is then replaced by two green triangles to form hexagon C.

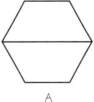

A   B   C

©1996 Cuisenaire Company of America, Inc.

In experimenting with different combinations of blocks, children quickly eliminate the orange square and the tan rhombus. They notice that after a square or a rhombus is put down, no other Pattern Block can be added that allows for the formation of a hexagon that is congruent to the yellow block. Children may try to flip or rotate their solutions to identify and weed out those that are the same. Although effective, this strategy is not foolproof in helping children to find duplicate combinations. For example, these two shapes appear to be different solutions but actually represent the same combination because each has two greens and two blues:

Children may decide that counting the number of each kind of block used in each solution is a good way to see if they have any duplicates. By recording the numbers of blocks in a table, children can readily spot combinations that are the same. A table or chart may also help children to consider additional possible combinations of blocks to try. This table shows the seven possible solutions numerically:

Green blocks	6	4	3	2	1	0	0
Blue blocks	0	1	0	2	1	3	0
Red blocks	0	0	1	0	1	0	2

This activity provides an ideal springboard for work with fractions. Specifically, it gives meaning to the addition of halves, thirds, and sixths. For example, the solution shown can be used to show 1/2 + 1/6 + 1/6 + 1/6 = 1. It can also be used to help children understand why 1/2 > 1/6 or why 3 x 1/6 = 1/2. Children's familiarity with these kinds of models provides them with concrete ways to think about and work with fractions.

CONGRUENT SHAPES

Getting Ready

What You'll Need

Pattern Blocks, about 40 per pair
Crayons
Scissors
Paste
Overhead Pattern Blocks (optional)

Overview

Children create a shape using four Pattern Blocks and then use other combinations or arrangements of blocks to build shapes that are congruent to the original. In this activity, children have the opportunity to:

◆ explore and use equivalences among shapes

◆ test shapes for congruence

◆ develop spatial visualization skills

The Activity

Introducing

◆ Show the class this arrangement of Pattern Blocks. Ask children to duplicate your design with their blocks.

◆ Now, ask children to make the same shape, but with a different combination or arrangement of blocks.

◆ Call on a few children to display their designs. Invite discussion about whether all the designs are the same size and shape.

◆ Explain that the designs form shapes that are *congruent*. Point out that this means they are the same size and same shape.

On Their Own

How many different ways can you make the same shape with Pattern Blocks?

- With a partner, choose 4 Pattern Blocks and make a design.

- Make sure that at least 1 complete side of each block touches 1 complete side of another block.

- Record your design by tracing it at the top of a piece of paper. Then color it in to show which block you used.

- Now try to make other designs that have the same shape and size as your original design. You may either use blocks that are different from the original design or use the same blocks in a different way.

- Find a way to check that the shape of each new design is congruent to the shape of your original design.

- Record each new design by tracing and coloring it on a separate sheet of paper.

- When you think you have found all the different ways to make your shape, cut out your designs and paste them below the original design.

The Bigger Picture

Thinking and Sharing

Post children's work and invite them to share their observations.

Use prompts like these to promote class discussion:

- What strategies did you use for making congruent shapes?

- How did you check that your shapes were really congruent?

- Do you think you have found all the possible ways to make your shape? Explain.

- What do you notice when you look at the posted designs?

- Which shapes were made in the greatest number of ways? Which shapes were made in the least number of ways? Why do you think this is so?

Writing

Ask children to explain how they knew that they had found all the different ways to make their shape.

Extending the Activity

1. Have children repeat the activity, this time using five Pattern Blocks to make a shape and five or fewer to make shapes congruent to the original.

2. Have children use six Pattern Blocks to make a shape and six or fewer to make shapes congruent to the original.

Where's the Mathematics?

In searching for different ways to make congruent shapes, children use spatial skills to find ways to make equivalent substitutions of the Pattern Blocks. Some children may start by decomposing the blocks in their original shape into two or more blocks that can be used to fill the same space filled by each original block. The sequence of shapes below shows one way that this might be done. Equivalences were used to make a substitution of two greens for a blue, then a blue and green for red, then two greens for a blue, and two greens for the last blue.

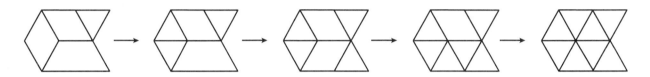

At this point, children need to use equivalences that involve the replacement of several smaller blocks with larger blocks to find other ways to build the same shape. For example, children may see that two groups of three green triangles can be replaced by two red trapezoids, as shown in A below. Other children may notice that each pair of triangles can be replaced with a blue parallelogram, as in B, or that six of the triangles can be replaced by a yellow hexagon, as in C.

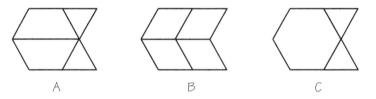

Some children may approach the problem by exploring all the different ways each set of four blocks can be arranged to make the same shape. The sequence below shows four ways to rearrange the same four blocks.

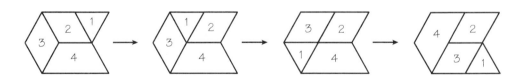

Children who have worked with filling outlines with Pattern Blocks or Tangrams may not rely as much on the relationship among the Pattern Blocks. These children will create the first design and then trace just its outline. This way they can try to fit different combinations of blocks within the outline without being influenced by the blocks that were first used. For example, the outline of the shape in the *Introducing* section would look like this:

As they continue to make new designs, children need to check that each new arrangement of blocks creates a shape that is indeed congruent to the original shape and that the new design is not a duplication of a design already made. Some children may not easily recognize duplication, especially in shapes that themselves have rotational symmetry. For example, using a logical sequence of equivalent substitutions, a child may make the following six designs, not realizing that shape H is the same arrangement as shape E, and shape I is the same arrangement as shape F.

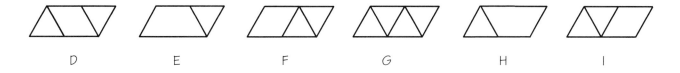

When children share their work, they may notice that some groups made shapes that could be designed in many more ways than could those of other groups. Children may realize that the number of different arrangements that can be made depends a lot on the size of the blocks chosen for the original shape. In general, the larger the blocks used, the greater the number of ways to make congruent shapes. Children may reason that this is because there are many more substitutions that can be made for a larger block, such as a yellow hexagon, than for a smaller block, such as a blue parallelogram.

This activity is filled with opportunities for children to strengthen their spatial reasoning and visualization ability. The skills needed to replace larger blocks equivalently with smaller ones, to replace smaller blocks equivalently with larger ones, to compare designs to check for duplication, and to compare shapes to check for congruence require different kinds of thought processes. These skills are important for children to develop and maintain and to be able to apply to other mathematical contexts.

HEXIAMONDS

- Spatial reasoning
- Congruence
- Transformational geometry

Getting Ready

What You'll Need

Pattern Block triangles, 24 per group

Pattern Block triangle paper, page 90

Scissors

Overhead Pattern Blocks (optional)

Overview

Children search to find all the different arrangements that can be made using six green Pattern Block triangles. In this activity, children have the opportunity to:

- ◆ devise strategies for finding shapes
- ◆ reinforce their understanding of congruence by using flips and rotations to compare shapes

Here's the problem!

How many "Hexiamonds" can you make?

Use six green triangles to find all the possible shapes that can be made.

The Activity

There are only two other arrangements that can be made using four triangles.

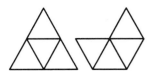

Introducing

- ◆ Display four green Pattern Block triangles, as shown below. Point out that at least one entire side of each triangle touches one entire side of another.

- ◆ Ask children to try to build a different arrangement using four green triangles.

- ◆ Call on several volunteers to display their shapes near yours.

- ◆ Ask children whether any of the arrangements displayed are the same shape. Ask them to explain how they know.

- ◆ Select two shapes that are congruent and show children how one can be flipped and/or rotated to look exactly like the other. Establish that these shapes are congruent and therefore are not considered different arrangements of the blocks.

On Their Own

How many different hexiamonds can you make?

- With your group, make as many different hexiamonds as you can. A hexiamond is a shape that can be made with 6 green Pattern Block triangles.

- Make sure that at least 1 complete side of each triangle in your hexiamonds touches 1 complete side of another triangle.

Okay

Not okay

Not okay

- Record each hexiamond on triangle paper and cut it out.

- Be ready to explain why you think you have found all the different hexiamonds that can be made.

The Bigger Picture

Thinking and Sharing

Create a class hexiamond chart by inviting volunteers, one at a time, to post one of their cutout shapes. Tell children that they may only post shapes that are different from those already posted. As each shape is added to the chart, have children check to see whether their group made the same shape. When the chart is complete, have them check for and remove any duplicates.

Use prompts like these to promote class discussion:

- Do you think that you have found all the possible hexiamonds? Explain.

- What strategies did you use to find new shapes?

- How do the shapes differ from one another?

- When you thought you were finished, did you sort your hexiamonds in a way that helped you see if any were missing? If so, explain.

Remind children that if one shape can be turned and/or rotated to look exactly like another, the two shapes are not to be considered different.

Extending the Activity

1. Suggest that children sort the 12 hexiamonds in various ways, such as by number of sides, as symmetrical or not, or as concave or convex.

2. Have children do the same investigation with the orange squares and/or with the blue parallelograms.

3. Ask children to prove or disprove this statement: *All hexiamonds have the same area and the same perimeter.*

Where's the Mathematics?

There are twelve different hexiamonds.

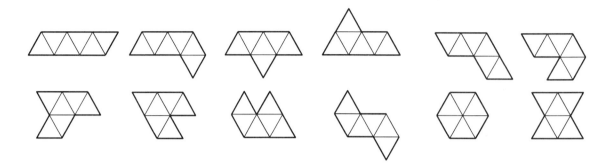

Many children may start by randomly arranging and rearranging triangles. At some point, when additional shapes are not obvious, children may begin to look for a way to organize their search. Some may first place six triangles in a row and move one or more triangles to different locations.

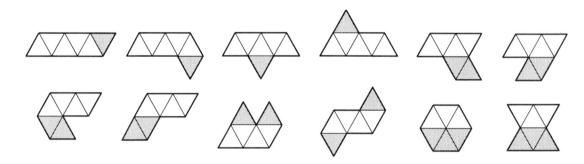

Other children may begin by making a hexagon, pulling out one triangle, then another triangle, and so on.

©1996 Cuisenaire Company of America, Inc.

Still others may notice that three green triangles make a trapezoid, that four make an equilateral triangle. Once they realize this, children can search for hexiamonds that contain these shapes. Children may even decide to sort what they find according to how many times a particular shape occurs.

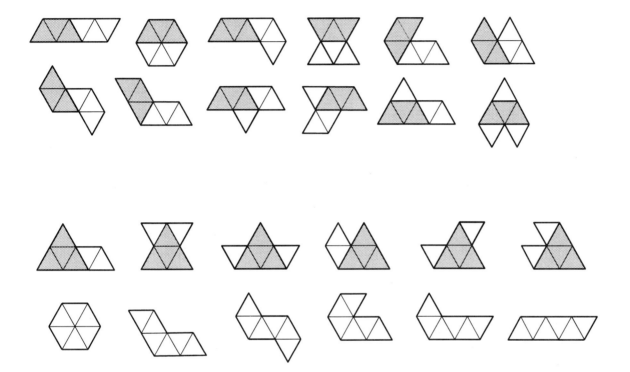

In testing for congruence, children have an opportunity to use transformational geometry in an informal setting. Whereas some children may simply "eyeball" the shapes, others may manipulate their blocks or cutout shapes to check whether they can be flipped or rotated to fit one on top of the other.

MAKE MY DESIGN

• Spatial visualization
• Properties of geometric figures

Getting Ready

What You'll Need

Pattern Blocks, 10 per child

Books or heavy folders to serve as barriers

Overhead Pattern Blocks (optional)

Overview

Children create Pattern Block designs and take turns describing the designs so that their partner can recreate them without seeing them. In this activity, children have the opportunity to:

♦ use clear and accurate language to describe geometric attributes and spatial relationships

♦ improve their listening and visualizations skills

♦ practice using effective questioning techniques

The Activity

Children's lists may include questions such as: How many blocks? What kinds of blocks? Do they touch each other? How? What does the overall shape look like?

Introducing

♦ Prepare a design using any four Pattern Blocks. Conceal it from the class.

♦ Tell children that you have made a Pattern Block design and that you would like to describe it so that they can make the same design without seeing yours.

♦ Ask children to brainstorm, first with a partner, then with the class, a list of questions they would like you to answer about your design.

♦ Using children's questions as a guide, describe your design and have children try to build it. Allow children to ask more questions if they need more information.

♦ Reveal your design and invite discussion. Together, recall words you used that helped children and words that confused them.

On Their Own

Can you describe a Pattern Block design so well that someone else can build your design without seeing it?

- Build a barrier between you and your partner to hide your designs.

- Make a design using 3 Pattern Blocks. Make sure that the blocks lie flat and that no blocks are on top of one another.

- Describe your design to your partner. Use words that will help your partner figure out how to make the same design.

- Your partner may ask you questions to get more information.

- When your partner is done, compare designs. If they are not alike, discuss why.

- Switch roles and repeat the activity. Use more than 3 blocks if you like.

- Continue to switch roles and repeat the activity. Think about how to improve your directions and your questions each time.

The Bigger Picture

Thinking and Sharing

Ask children to talk about their experiences giving directions and recreating each other's designs.

Use prompts such as these to promote class discussion:

- Would you rather be the person who describes or the person who tries to figure out the design? Tell why.

- What was easy to describe about the designs?

- What was difficult to describe? Why?

- What kinds of questions were helpful to ask?

- Were some of the descriptions unhelpful? Why?

- Which words sometimes caused confusion? How so?

Writing

Have children work with a partner to make a Pattern Block design and to write a list of directions that other children could follow to make the same design.

1. Work with children to make a class vocabulary list of words that are helpful for describing Pattern Block designs; for example, *right, left, above, edges, vertices, parallel,* and *perpendicular.* Then have children go back and try the activity again using words from this list.

2. Have children try this variation of the activity: The partner who makes the design does not describe it. Instead, the partner who is trying to

Teacher Talk

Where's the Mathematics?

As children work through this activity, they become aware of the importance of effective communication and the need for accurate geometric language. They also notice the geometric attributes of the shapes in their designs. Words such as *sides, corners (vertices), edges, faces, surfaces, adjacent,* and *parallel* become helpful in adding clarity to children's descriptions.

Children should recognize that the goal of the activity is not to try to trick or mislead their partner but rather to provide clear, accurate descriptions that will enable their partner to build an exact replica of the original design. As they take turns in the two roles, children learn to identify the kinds of descriptions that are most helpful. They recognize that some words communicate ideas more clearly than others. For example, if one partner describes a design as "two red trapezoids with a blue parallelogram in the middle," the other partner may build any one of these designs:

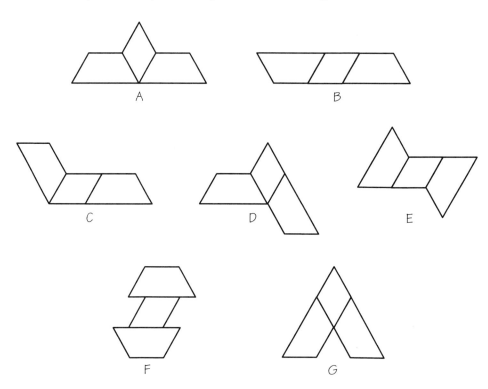

figure out the design must ask questions until he or she has enough information to successfully build it.

3. Ask pairs of children to make a Pattern Block design, record it on triangle paper, color it, and cut it out. Have them write a clear description of their design on an index card. Post the recorded designs and descriptions separately and challenge children to match the descriptions with the designs.

However, once the need for more detail becomes apparent, children must find effective ways to communicate how the blocks are adjoined. For example, if design A is the original design, the child describing the design might add, in his or her own words, that the slanted sides of the two trapezoids touch adjacent sides of the parallelogram and that the longest sides of the trapezoids together form one long side of the overall design. If design B is the original design, the child describing the design might add that the slanted sides of the trapezoids touch sides of the parallelogram that are parallel to each other, forming an overall design that itself is a parallelogram.

Children may find that their success with the activity also depends on their ability to ask good questions. Some children may learn that by using effective questioning techniques, they are able to obtain information that is more useful to them than some of the clues provided by their partner. The questions children ask can help both partners develop better descriptions for future designs.

As children build more intricate designs using larger numbers of blocks, the language they need in order to describe the designs may become more complicated and the number of clues needed may greatly increase. When designs are compared, children may be surprised to discover that descriptions they had considered adequate may also accurately describe a design that is different from the original. In discussing how the description could have been improved so that it fits only the one design, children must focus on the characteristics that differentiate the two designs. The ability to recognize and accurately describe these differences is a valuable skill that children will use throughout their study of geometry.

ONLY TWO BLOCKS

Getting Ready

What You'll Need

Pattern Blocks, about 20 per pair

Crayons

Scissors

Overhead Pattern Blocks (optional)

Overview

Children try to create as many different shapes as possible using combinations of two different Pattern Blocks. They then record and sort the shapes they have made. In this activity, children have the opportunity to:

◆ discover different geometric shapes

◆ explore congruence among shapes

◆ sort and classify shapes

The Activity

Point out that this shape does not follow the rule because the side of the triangle touches only part of the side of the trapezoid.

Explain that one way to check whether shapes are congruent is to trace them, cut them out, and put one on top of the other. If they can be made to match exactly, they are congruent.

Introducing

◆ Let children use Pattern Blocks to investigate this question: If you put a green triangle and a red trapezoid together so that one entire side of one touches one entire side of the other, what shapes can you make?

◆ When children feel they are ready, call on a volunteer to display one shape. Identify it as either a triangle or a parallelogram.

◆ Have another volunteer show a different shape and identify it.

◆ Establish that the triangle and the parallelogram are the only different shapes that can be made. Explain that the parallelograms shown below are not different because they can be flipped or rotated to look exactly the same. Confirm that these parallelograms are therefore congruent.

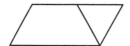  

©1996 Cuisenaire Company of America, Inc.

On Their Own

How many different shapes can you make using 2 different Pattern Blocks?

- Choose any 2 different Pattern Blocks. Working with a partner, make as many different shapes as you can using these 2 blocks. For each shape, make sure that 1 entire side of each block touches 1 entire side of another block.

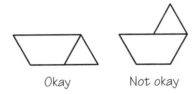

Okay   Not okay

- Record your shapes by tracing and coloring them. Then cut them out.

- Now do the same with other combinations of 2 different blocks.

- When you think you have found all the possible shapes that can be made, find a way to sort them.

The Bigger Picture

Thinking and Sharing

Ask the pairs to describe how they sorted their shapes. Then suggest that, as a class, children arrange their shapes on a chart according to the number of sides the shapes have. Post one cutout shape and have children suggest an appropriate label for that column. Invite children from each group to come up and post different shapes that belong in that column. Continue in this way, creating new columns as needed, until all the different shapes are displayed.

Use prompts such as these to promote class discussion:

- How did you go about finding the different shapes?

- What did you notice about the shapes you made?

- How did you convince yourself that you had found all possible combinations of two blocks?

- What did you discover about shapes made with the red trapezoid?

- What did you do to check for congruent shapes?

Children familiar with polygon names may want to use those names for labels. Other children may suggest labels such as "4 sides" or "5 sides."

Extending the Activity

Ask children to repeat the activity using three different Pattern Blocks. Have children predict how the number of possible shapes will compare with the

Where's the Mathematics?

It is not likely that individual pairs will find every one of the 23 possible different shapes. However, in making the attempt, children gain valuable experience in discovering ways to compare shapes for congruence and in classifying the shapes they find.

In their search for different shapes, some children may find it helpful to create a list to which they can refer to ensure that they are considering all combinations of two different blocks. This table shows one way to do this:

Ways to Combine Two Different Pattern Blocks

yellow–red	red–blue	blue–green	green–orange	orange–tan
yellow–blue	red–green	blue–orange	green–tan	
yellow–green	red–orange	blue–tan		
yellow–orange	red–tan			
yellow–tan				

As children experiment to find the different shapes, they may notice that whereas most combinations of blocks fit together to make only one shape, combinations involving the red trapezoid yield more than one shape: The yellow-red combination forms two shapes, red-blue forms three, red-green forms two, red-orange forms two, and red-tan forms three. Children may also discover that the blue-tan combination forms two different shapes. Children may be able to explain that these combinations form more than one shape because the red, blue, and tan shapes have angles that are not all congruent.

The next table shows how the shapes can be organized according to number of sides.

number that can be made with only two blocks. Suggest that children sort the shapes made with three blocks and create a new chart.

3-Sided Shapes (Triangles)	4-Sided Shapes (Quadrilaterals)	5-Sided Shapes (Pentagons)	6-Sided Shapes (Hexagons)	7-Sided Shapes (Heptagons)	8-Sided Shapes (Octagons)

As children examine the table, they can compare and discuss the shapes in each column. They may notice that there are many more 6-sided shapes. Some children may recognize that this is because four of the six Pattern Block shapes are 4-sided, and when they are adjoined, two of their total of eight sides become internal to the new shape, leaving six sides exposed. This often results in a shape with six sides. Children may also note that most of the shapes are concave, even though they are made from Pattern Blocks shapes, which are convex.

RECOVER THE SYMMETRY

Getting Ready

What You'll Need

Pattern Blocks, about 30 per pair

Mirrors, 1 per pair (optional)

Overhead Pattern Blocks (optional)

Overview

In this game for two players, children create symmetrical designs with Pattern Blocks, disturb the symmetry, and then challenge a partner to restore symmetry to their design. In this activity, children have the opportunity to:

♦ verify that a design has line symmetry

♦ develop spatial visualization skills

The Activity

Remind children that a shape has line symmetry if it can be "folded in half" in such a way so that one half fits exactly on top of the other half. Point out that mirrors can be used to check for line symmetry. By holding a mirror along the line of symmetry of a design, children should be able to see in the reflection what the other half of the design looks like.

Introducing

♦ Before working with the class, build two identical shapes symmetrical in both color and shape. Then move two blocks in one of the shapes to make it asymmetrical. For example:

♦ Display both shapes and identify them as being symmetrical and asymmetrical, respectively. Invite children to make observations about the symmetrical shape. Establish that it has line symmetry and point out the location of the line of symmetry.

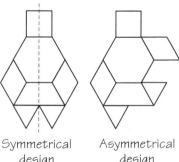

Symmetrical design   Asymmetrical design

♦ Have children suggest how they might move two blocks in the asymmetrical shape to make it symmetrical. Call on one or more volunteers to try this, and let children consider the results.

On Their Own

Play *Recover the Symmetry!*

Here are the rules:

1. This is a game for 2 players.

2. Together, players build a symmetrical design using 12 Pattern Blocks. The design should be symmetrical in both shape and color.

Okay

Symmetrical in both shape and color

Not okay

Symmetrical in shape but not in color

3. Players can use a mirror to check the symmetry of the design. They can look for other lines of symmetry by turning the mirror in different directions.

4. Next, one player looks away while the other player moves 3 blocks so that the design is no longer symmetrical.

5. The player who wasn't looking then tries to move 3 blocks to make the design symmetrical again.

6. After the symmetry has been recovered, players talk over these questions with each other: Is the new design symmetrical? Were the same blocks moved to recover the symmetry? Is the final design the same as the original one?

• Play several rounds of *Recover the Symmetry*.

• Be ready to talk about your games.

The Bigger Picture

Thinking and Sharing

Invite children to talk about their games.

Use prompts like these to promote class discussion:

♦ Which was easier, creating the original design or recovering the symmetry? Why?

♦ What did you notice during the game?

♦ Did you ever discover more than one line of symmetry in a design? If so, describe how this happened.

♦ What helped you decide how to move the blocks to recover the symmetry?

♦ When you made an asymmetrical shape symmetrical, did you recreate the original shape or did you find a new one? Why do you think this happened?

Extending the Activity

1. Have each pair of children make two identical symmetrical designs using Pattern Blocks, trace the outline of each, and draw in the line of symmetry. Then have children exchange outlines with another pair and use Pattern Blocks to fill one outline with a design that is symmetrical in color and the other with a design that is not. Have children compare the designs and discuss the differences.

Where's the Mathematics?

In this activity, children work with line symmetry, which is the exact correspondence of form and configuration on opposite sides of an imaginary line. A shape with form symmetry may or may not have color symmetry. The design on the left has form symmetry and color symmetry whereas the design on the right has form symmetry but not color symmetry.

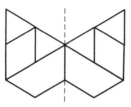 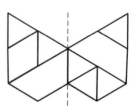

Some children may form their designs by first drawing a line of symmetry and then placing blocks in reflection positions on each side of the line. For example, children might first place the red trapezoids as shown, then the blue parallelograms, then the orange squares, and so on.

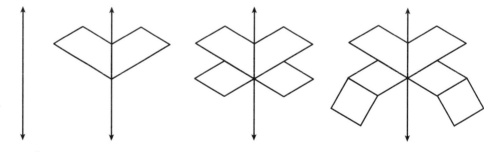

Line of symmetry

Children who are able to visualize lines of symmetry within each of the Pattern Blocks may create designs similar to the one in the *Introducing* section of the activity. In these designs, the line of symmetry passes *through* the blocks.

After the discussion of symmetry in the *Introducing* section, most children will probably opt to create a design with a vertical line of symmetry, although some may decide to work with a horizontal line of symmetry.

2. Ask children to make a symmetrical design using 12 Pattern Blocks and then move four blocks from that design to make a new symmetrical design. Have them continue to create new symmetrical designs in this way, record each design, and see how many different symmetrical designs can be built.

Those children who look for additional lines of symmetry and feel motivated to adjust their symmetrical designs may be able to come up with designs that have both vertical and horizontal lines of symmetry. Still others who have had experience with analyzing figures for symmetry may form designs with more than two lines of symmetry.

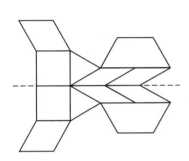

Horizontal line of symmetry

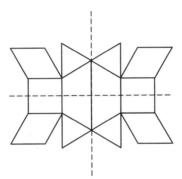

Two lines of symmetry

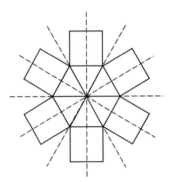

More than two lines of symmetry

When children first play *Recover the Symmetry*, it is likely that the final design will be identical to their original design. As they become more comfortable with the idea of symmetry, they may look for ways to recover the symmetry by forming a new design. Here is an example of how such a game might play out. Figure A shows the original design, figure B shows an asymmetrical design that results from moving one red, one blue, and one green block, and figure C shows a symmetrical design, different from the first, that results from moving one red, one green, and one blue block.

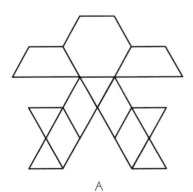

A

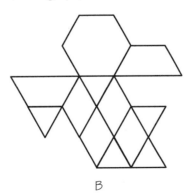

B

C

RIDDLE MAKERS

- Properties of geometric figures
- Spatial visualization
- Deductive reasoning

Getting Ready

What You'll Need

Pattern Blocks, about 25 per pair

Small paper bags, 1 per pair

1 small bag containing 1 green triangle, 1 blue parallelogram, and 1 red trapezoid, stapled shut

Overview

Children create riddles that provide clues about Pattern Blocks that they have hidden in a paper bag. They then try to solve each other's riddles. In this activity, children have the opportunity to:

- develop understanding of geometric properties
- communicate about mathematical concepts
- use logical reasoning skills
- explore spatial relationships among polygons

The Activity

After each clue, allow time for children to consider blocks that fit the clues and could be possible solutions.

Children might find it helpful to think about clues in a more general way; for example, number, color, shape of blocks, and relative sizes.

Introducing

- Display your sealed Riddle Bag. Tell children that you will give clues to help them figure out exactly which Pattern Blocks are in the bag.
- Give the first clue: *The Pattern Blocks in the bag can form a design that is the same size and shape as the yellow hexagon.* Have children look for blocks that match this clue.
- Tell children to work with this clue next: *There is one red block.*
- Now present the last clue: *There are three different kinds of Pattern Blocks in the bag.*
- When they are ready, have children display their solutions. Then reveal the contents of the Riddle Bag.
- Discuss what qualities make a good clue. Establish that each new clue should bring the solution closer.
- Ask children to picture a Riddle Bag that contains two red trapezoids and three blue parallelograms. Ask partners to come up with at least two clues for a riddle about those blocks.
- Call on volunteers to share their clues.

On Their Own

Can you think of some really good clues to use in your own Pattern Block riddle?

- With a partner, choose up to 6 Pattern Blocks to write clues about.

- Examine your blocks. Notice things about them.

- Decide on 3 to 5 clues for your riddle and write them down. For example, if you choose 2 green blocks and 2 blue blocks, your riddle might say:

  Together the blocks form a hexagon the same size and shape as
      the yellow Pattern Block.
  There are 2 different kinds of blocks in the bag.
  There is the same number of each type of block.

- Talk about each clue. Is it too hard? Does it give away the riddle too soon?

- When you have all your clues, test your riddle and make sure it works. Then put your Pattern Blocks in the paper bag, close it, and clip the riddle to the bag.

- Exchange Riddle Bags with another pair and try to solve their riddle. Then look in the bag to check your solution.

The Bigger Picture

Thinking and Sharing

Invite children to talk about how they wrote and tested their riddles and how they solved the riddles written by others.

Use prompts like these to promote class discussion:

- What did you notice about writing riddle clues?

- What words helped you as you created clues?

- After reading a clue, were there any blocks you knew for certain were going to be in the bag? Why?

- Did you sometimes need only a few of the clues to solve a riddle? Explain.

- Is it possible to have different clues that describe the same set of blocks? Explain.

- Was it easier to solve or to create riddles? Why?

Writing

Have children explain how they could write clues to describe Pattern Blocks without using colors or names of geometric shapes. (For example, a square could be described as a four-sided shape with four equal sides and four square corners.)

Extending the Activity

1. Ask children to write riddles that contain extra, unnecessary clues. Have children exchange their riddles, solve them, and discuss which clues can be omitted. (You might want to model this activity beforehand.)

2. Have children create and solve riddles using other manipulatives, such as Cuisenaire® Rods and Color Tiles.

Teacher Talk

Where's the Mathematics?

Children may well find solving riddles easier than writing them. Even though children may feel a certain comfort level in using their own words to communicate their ideas, they soon realize that they must take special care that their written clues really provide the information they are meant to convey. The task of writing clues helps children to become aware of the importance of using precise language and geometric vocabulary.

As they write and test their riddles, children may discover and use certain types of clues. These clues may include information about total number of blocks, relative number of blocks, shape or color of the blocks, and how blocks can be arranged. One strategy children can use is to begin with general clues ("There are eight blocks.") and end with more specific clues ("There are twice as many yellows as reds.").

When children compare their riddle-writing experiences, they may be surprised to find that two different riddles can describe the same set of blocks. Here are two examples:

There are 3 blocks.
They are all different.
If you combine the 2 larger shapes, you get a shape that can be covered exactly by 8 of the smallest shape.

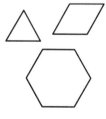

There are 3 blocks.
One is 3 times the size of one of the others.
One is twice the size of one of the others.
There is no red block.

In attempting to solve riddles, children develop their own strategies for dealing with individual clues. Some solve the clues one by one, in order, and evaluate the possibilities as they go. For example, in the riddle in the *Introducing* part of the activity, children may first try to collect all the combinations of blocks that can be used to form a shape congruent to the yellow hexagon. This might involve combinations using the same kind of block (for instance, six green triangles) or combinations using different kinds of

3. Invite children to solve this Pattern Block riddle:

> There are 3 blocks in the bag.
> Each block has a different number of sides.
> Each block has sides that are equal in length.
> The 3 shapes can be covered by 9 triangles.
> What's in the bag?

---

blocks (for instance, one blue parallelogram and four green triangles). In addition to making their combinations, children may also be able to conclude from the first clue that the orange and tan blocks can't be used. After the second clue, children can eliminate all the combinations that do not have a red block. After the third clue, children can again use the process of elimination, ruling out combinations that don't consist of three different kinds of blocks, and arrive at the correct combination of blocks.

In solving more challenging riddles, some children may prefer to read through all of the clues before deciding on a strategy. Here is an example of a more involved riddle that children might write or solve:

> There are only quadrilaterals in the bag.
> All the blocks can be put together to
> form 2 hexagons, each congruent
> to the yellow block.
> There are 5 blocks in all.
> There are no yellow blocks.

Some children may first read all the clues and then try to satisfy the ones that seem most important, most difficult, or most useful. After reading the riddle, children may decide that the second clue is the hardest to satisfy and start their search for solutions by finding combinations of blocks that can be used to form the two hexagons.

Children may also use the strategy of combining clues in their minds. For example, children might combine the first two clues in the riddle above and use only quadrilaterals to form the two hexagon shapes.

Some children may learn to look for clues that give unnecessary information and eliminate those clues. For example, the last clue in the riddle above is unnecessary, since the first clue indicates that there are no yellow blocks. Because there is seemingly less information to synthesize, children may feel that they have made the riddle easier to solve by eliminating unnecessary clues.

SIZE THEM UP!

Getting Ready

What You'll Need

Pattern Blocks (no orange or tan), about 10 per child

Scissors

Paste

Overhead Pattern Blocks (optional)

Overview

Children make shapes with Pattern Blocks, trace the outlines of their shapes, and arrange the outlines in what they perceive to be size order. They then look for different ways to check that they have ordered their shapes correctly. In this activity, children have the opportunity to:

◆ explore the concept of area

◆ develop a variety of ways to compare the areas of different shapes

◆ use equivalencies among shapes to determine relative size

The Activity

Introducing

◆ Remind children that *area* refers to the amount of space inside a shape.

◆ Display these two Pattern Block shapes.

◆ Ask children which shape they think has the greater area and why.

On Their Own

> ### How can you compare the areas of Pattern Block designs?
>
> - Work in a group. Each of you choose 6 Pattern Blocks and make a design. You may use any combination of green, blue, red, and yellow blocks.
>
> - Trace the outline of your design on white paper and cut it out.
>
> - Put your outline together with the others made by your group. Work together to arrange the shapes in order from the one you think has the smallest area to the one you think has the largest area.
>
> - Now find a way to check that you have ordered the shapes correctly. You may use any method you can think of.
>
> - Paste your shapes in order on a large sheet of paper.
>
> - Be ready to explain how you know your shapes are in the right order.

The Bigger Picture

Thinking and Sharing

Have children post their work and invite them to discuss what happened during the activity.

Use prompts such as these to promote class discussion:

- What kinds of things did you consider when trying to put your shapes in order from smallest to largest?

- What was the hardest part about trying to order your shapes?

- Did you think that any of your shapes had the same area? If so, what made you think so?

- How does the area of your largest shape compare to that of your smallest shape?

- What method(s) did you use to check that the shapes were in the correct order?

- Look at the posted shapes. Are there any that you think may be out of order? If so, which ones and why?

Extending the Activity

Have children work in pairs to create a Pattern Block design of a given object using any combination and number of green, blue, red, and yellow Pattern Blocks. For example, everyone might make butterflies, rocketships, or flowers. Have children record their design on triangle paper, color it in, and cut it out. Then have them compare their designs and try to order them from smallest to largest.

Where's the Mathematics?

In this activity, children have an opportunity to make the connection between area and what they perceive to be the size of a shape. As they compare their outlines, they focus on the amount of space contained within. In some instances, it may be obvious that one shape has more space inside than another. However, in other cases, the differences in shape may not allow for an easy comparison. For example, it may be difficult to compare two shapes like the ones below, where one is fairly compact and the other is elongated.

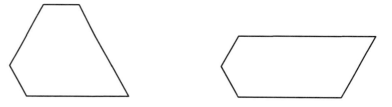

Some children may think that elongated shapes have greater areas than compact shapes. These children may be influenced by the relative sizes of the perimeters. While it is true that if two different shapes have the same area, the more elongated shape will have a larger perimeter, it is not necessarily true that shapes with longer perimeters have larger areas.

Children may also have difficulty making comparisons between the relative areas of concave shapes and convex shapes. The protruding parts of concave shapes may give children the impression of greater area. For example, in comparing the shapes below, children may be inclined to choose the concave shape as the larger, even though both of these outlines are made from the same six Pattern Blocks.

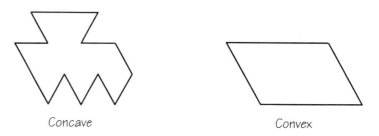

Concave   Convex

There are many different ways that children may try to verify that they have ordered their shapes correctly. Some may try to compare the areas by placing one cutout shape on top of another and looking to see if one extends beyond the other in one or more places. Other children may use one or more Pattern Blocks to compare areas in a similar way. For example, children might fit yellow hexagons into two outlines and try to judge which outline has more or less uncovered space.

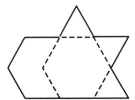 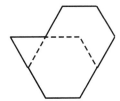

Children may use this same method for larger shapes, covering each shape with several Pattern Blocks.

Children who are familiar with the Pattern Block equivalencies may try to rebuild the designs by filling in the outlines with different blocks. They may then compare the two sets of blocks used to form the shapes, matching equivalent blocks to see which shape is made from more blocks (or parts of blocks) than the other. Other children may exchange the blocks they used to rebuild the shapes for equivalent blocks so that they can compare the areas in terms of the same size block. For example, to compare the areas of the shapes below, children may investigate to see which set of blocks can be exchanged for more yellow hexagons. Using equivalencies, children would find that whereas the blocks in A can be exchanged for two yellow hexagons, the blocks in B are equivalent in area to two yellow hexagons plus a green triangle.

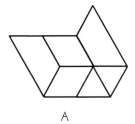 

A   B

Some children may try to measure the space inside the outlines using a common unit of area measurement. For example, children may try to fill the outlines with green triangles and order them according to the number of triangles that make up each shape. In doing this, children acquire a way to represent area numerically. For some children, this may be the only way for them to be convinced that they have ordered their shapes correctly. This method also exposes children to the use of non-standard units for measurement, an important concept in mathematics.

SPINEY AND OTHER CREATURES

- Organizing and interpreting data
- Addition/multiplication
- Growth patterns
- Predicting with patterns

Getting Ready

What You'll Need

Pattern Blocks, about 50 per pair

Crayons

Overhead Pattern Blocks (optional)

Overview

Children build Pattern Block creatures that grow in predictable ways. They then try to predict what their creatures will look like and how many blocks it will take to build them after seven stages of growth. In this activity, children have the opportunity to:

- ◆ discover patterns
- ◆ use patterns to make predictions
- ◆ use patterns to make generalizations

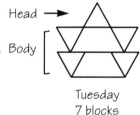

The Activity

To offer extra practice, you may want children to predict what some other creatures will look like on their third day of growth. Refer to Pincher and Pyramid Pete, both shown in Where's the Mathematics?.

Introducing

- ◆ Tell the class that you have invented a Pattern Block creature named Spiney. Explain that Spiney grows very fast and in a predictable way.

- ◆ Using Pattern Blocks, display Spiney as he looked on Monday and Tuesday.

Head →

Body [

Monday
4 blocks

Head →

Body [

Tuesday
7 blocks

- ◆ Invite volunteers to describe how Spiney grew from one day to the next.

- ◆ Ask children to work with a partner to build Spiney the way he would look on Wednesday.

- ◆ Have children share their solutions and describe their reasoning. Establish that Spiney grew by three blocks from day to day and that it takes ten blocks to build him the way he would look on Wednesday.

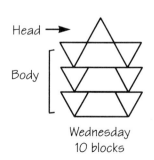

Head →

Body [

Wednesday
10 blocks

On Their Own

Can you create a growing Pattern Block creature and predict what it will look like on the seventh day?

- With a partner, create and name your own Pattern Block creature. Be sure to make a creature that can grow in a predictable way. This means there must be a pattern to the way the creature grows.

- Make a drawing of what your creature looks like on each of its first three days of life—Monday, Tuesday, and Wednesday. Record the number of blocks used for each day.

- Now figure out what your creature will look like on the seventh day, Sunday. Also figure out how many blocks you will need to build it. You can use blocks, a chart, or any other method for finding your answer.

- On a separate sheet of paper, draw your creature as it will look on Sunday. Write how many blocks it will take to build. Then, turn it over, keeping your drawing hidden.

- Exchange creature drawings that tell the number of blocks needed for Monday, Tuesday, and Wednesday with another pair of classmates. See if you can draw what their creature will look like and how many blocks it will need on Sunday, the seventh day.

- Compare your results with those of your classmates.

The Bigger Picture

Thinking and Sharing

Invite children to share their experiences, both in creating and growing their own creature and in working with another pair's creature.

Use prompts like these to promote class discussion:

- Was it easy to create a creature that could grow in predictable ways? Explain why or why not.

- How did you decide how to make your creature "grow" during its first three days?

- What strategies did you discover for figuring out what the creatures would look like on Sunday?

- Did patterns help you in any way? If so, how?

- Can you think of a way to figure out what your creature will look like on any given day and how many blocks you would need to build it? If you can, describe your method.

Writing

Have children explain why it is not necessary to actually build the creature on each day to figure out what size it will be on the seventh or even the fourteenth day.

Where's the Mathematics?

Children who are new to the idea of creating growth patterns will probably build creatures similar to Spiney in the sense that they grow by adding a constant number of blocks each day. Here are the first three days of growth for a creature called Pincher.

 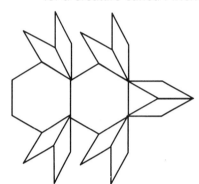 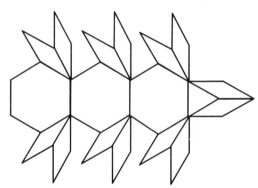

Children who make creatures such as Pincher may prefer to actually build or draw pictures of their creature on each day of growth and count the number of blocks used for each day. Children who record their creatures on a chart may be able to see patterns. Here is a partial chart of Pincher's first three days of growth.

Pincher's Growth

DAY	1	2	3	4	5	6	7	
BLOCKS	8	13	18					

Children may be able to conclude from the chart that Pincher gains five blocks each day. Repeated addition using 5 is one way to find the number of blocks for successive days: on the fourth day Pincher has 18 + 5 or 23 blocks; on the fifth day, 23 + 5 or 28 blocks; on the sixth day, 28 + 5 or 33 blocks; and on the seventh day, 33 + 5 or 38 blocks.

Based on the discussion of Spiney in the *Introducing* part of the activity, children may wish to think of their creature as having a head section that stays the same and a body section that grows. Children who focus on the kinds of blocks in each stage of growth may analyze Pincher this way: "The number of yellows is always the same as the number of days, and the number of tans in the body section is always four times the number of yellows. That means that on the fourth day, there are 4 yellow blocks and 4 x 4 or 16 tan blocks in the body section. Adding these to the 3 blocks in the head section gives a total of 23 blocks for the fourth day." Continuing this line of reasoning, on the seventh day, there are 7 yellow blocks, 28 tan body-section blocks, and 3 head-section blocks, for a total of 38 blocks.

Extending the Activity

Invite children to figure out the growth of their creatures for a two- or four-week period. Ask them to draw the creature at its oldest.

Children who focus on the total number of blocks added at each stage may think along these lines: "The number of blocks in the head section is always 3. The number of blocks in the body section is 5 on the first day, 2 x 5 or 10 on the second day, and 3 x 5 or 15 on the third day. That means that on the seventh day, the body section has 7 x 5 or 35 blocks and the head section has 3 blocks. That makes a total of 38 blocks on the seventh day." Children who are more advanced and can generalize may be able to draw this conclusion: "To find the total number of blocks for any day, I multiply the number of the day by 5 and add 3 to the answer."

Instead of adding a constant number of blocks at each stage of growth, some children may make creatures with growth patterns that involve adding larger and larger numbers of blocks. Such a creature might be similar to Pyramid Pete shown here:

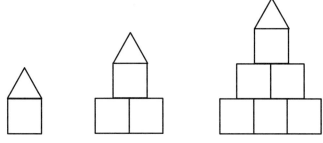

In Pyramid Pete's growth pattern, there are 2 blocks on the first day—1 "head" block and 1 "body" block. Then 2 blocks are added on the second day, 3 are added on the third day, and so on. By continuing to add numbers of blocks that correspond to the number of days of growth, children can figure out that on the seventh day, there are 2 + 2 + 3 + 4 + 5 + 6 + 7 or 29 blocks.

Sometimes there are additional interesting patterns of numbers involved in growth patterns like the one for Pyramid Pete. If children look at the creature as a head section with 1 block and a growing body section—1 on the first day, 3 on the second day, 6 on the third day, 10 on the fourth day, and so on—they have an opportunity to discover the set of triangular numbers—1, 3, 6, 10, 15, 21, 28—in the number of orange blocks on each day of growth.

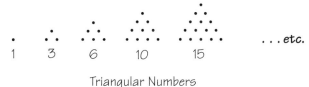

Triangular Numbers

SPINEY AND OTHER CREATURES ♦ Pattern Blocks ♦ Grades 3-4

THE LAST BLOCK

- Spatial visualization
- Properties of geometric figures
- Game strategies

Getting Ready

What You'll Need

Pattern Blocks, 50 per pair, with no orange or tan blocks

The Last Block game board, page 93

Overhead Pattern Blocks/Overhead transparency of *The Last Block* game board (optional)

Overview

In this game for two or four players, children take turns placing Pattern Blocks on a hexagonal game board. The winner is the player who places the last block on the board. In this activity, children have the opportunity to:

- develop strategic and logical thinking
- explore spatial relationships
- recognize relationships among areas of different shapes

The Activity

You may want to show one or more examples of moves that are not allowed.

 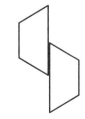

Introducing

- Tell children that they will be playing a Pattern Block game called *The Last Block.*
- Distribute game boards to each pair of children and explain the game rules given in *On Their Own.*
- Emphasize that at least one side of each block placed on the board must touch one complete side of a block that is already on the game board.
- Demonstrate by playing a partial game of *The Last Block*, either by yourself or with a volunteer.

On Their Own

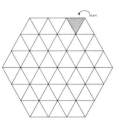

Play *The Last Block!*

Here are the rules.

1. This is a game for 2 or 4 players. The object is to be the player who places the last Pattern Block on *The Last Block* game board.

2. The first player places a green triangle on the space marked "Start."

3. Players take turns placing a Pattern Block on the board. At least 1 side of each new block must touch at least 1 complete side of a block that is already on the board.

4. The player who covers the last open space wins.

- Play several games of *The Last Block.* Take turns going first.

- Be ready to talk about good moves and bad moves.

The Bigger Picture

Thinking and Sharing

Invite children to talk about their games and describe some of the thinking they did.

Use prompts like these to promote class discussion:

- What kinds of things did you think about when planning your moves?
- Are there certain blocks you like to use at the beginning of the game? at the end? Why?
- Did you make any move that you then wanted to take back? Explain.
- What strategies did you discover to help you win and to keep your opponent from winning?

Extending the Activity

1. Have children play the game with this change in the rules: The player who covers the last space loses. Ask children to compare their strategy for this game with the strategy in the original game.

2. Have children design their own game boards. Invite children to exchange their game boards with others.

3. Have children choose 12 blocks to use before starting the game. After they have played the game several times, have partners discuss whether each person made good choices and why.

Where's the Mathematics?

When first playing *The Last Block*, many children will simply concentrate on covering the game board quickly by using larger blocks first and then using smaller blocks to cover the remaining spaces. Others may feel challenged to explore the different ways in which blocks can be placed on the game board. No matter what their approach, children have an opportunity to explore area relationships in an informal environment. Since the game board is made up of shapes congruent to the green triangle, children can see that the Pattern Blocks being used all relate in area to the green triangle; that is, the blue parallelogram is equivalent to two green triangles, the red trapezoid is equivalent to three green triangles, and the yellow hexagon is equivalent to six green triangles.

After playing several rounds, children will be able to begin to focus on winning strategies. They may come to realize that the winner will be the person who can analyze the remaining moves after most of the spaces on the game board have been covered. For example, below is a partial game board with four remaining spaces. There are two people playing, and it is Player 1's turn. Player 1 has a number of options from which to choose. If Player 1 places a green triangle on either a or d, there would remain a space the size of a red trapezoid, and Player 2 would win by placing the trapezoid. If Player 1 places a green triangle on b, Player 2 may place a green triangle on c or d, forcing two more plays. Player 2 may use a similar strategy if Player 1 places a green triangle on c. However, if Player 1 places a blue parallelogram on b and c, Player 2 would be forced to play a green triangle, leaving one last space to cover, and Player 1 would win.

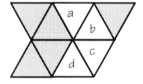

As the value of planning ahead becomes apparent, some children may decide that this is a good strategy: "When we get near the end of a game, I have to place the blocks so that there are an even number of possible moves left. That leaves one move for my opponent and one move for me, another move for my opponent and another move for me, and so on. Continuing this way, I will always get to place the last block and win." This thinking can be adapted for cases in which there are four players, although it is far more difficult to carry out: "I must try to make sure that the number of possible moves remaining is a multiple of four."

Below is another example of a partial game board with five remaining spaces, some adjacent, some not. There are two people playing, and it is Player 1's turn. Player 1 must ensure that there are an even number of remaining moves after his or her move. One way to ensure a win is to place a red trapezoid; that leaves two nonadjacent spaces to be covered. Another way to win would be to place a green triangle over the middle of the uncovered trapezoid shape; that leaves four nonadjacent spaces to be covered. If, however, Player 1 were to place a blue parallelogram, that would leave an odd number of nonadjacent spaces (3), and Player 2 would win.

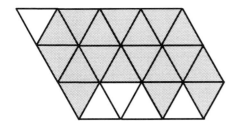

The Last Block requires children to use logical reasoning skills and strategic thinking to play well. As they test different strategies and plan ways to outwit their opponent, children develop thinking skills that will help them not only to become better game players but also to become more creative problem solvers.

TILING

Getting Ready

What You'll Need

Pattern Blocks, about 60 per pair

Overview

Children investigate which two-color combinations of Pattern Blocks can be used to tile a surface. In this activity, children have the opportunity to:

- begin to develop an understanding of tessellation
- develop spatial visualization skills
- examine tessellating designs for symmetry

The Activity

Introducing

- Ask children, working in pairs, to take a handful of green triangles and see if they can fit them together on a flat surface so that no space remains between pieces.
- Invite a few volunteers to report what they found.
- Explain that this way of putting shapes together is called *tessellating.*
- Assign each pair of children one of the other five Pattern Blocks and ask them to find out if their assigned shape tessellates.
- Let each pair in turn tell the class what they discovered. Children should find that each Pattern Block tessellates.

On Their Own

> **Can you find out which combinations of 2 Pattern Blocks can be used to tessellate a surface?**
>
> - With a partner, look for combinations of 2 different Pattern Blocks that will tessellate. Do this by seeing if you can cover a sheet of paper with the 2 kinds of blocks so that there are no spaces between the blocks.
>
> - Record which combinations of 2 blocks tessellate and which do not.
>
> - Continue until you have tried every combination of 2 blocks.
>
> - Select your favorite combination of tessellating blocks and use them to tessellate the sheet of paper. Leave this design in place.
>
> - Be ready to explain how you know you have found all the combinations that tessellate.

The Bigger Picture

Thinking and Sharing

Invite children to walk around the room and examine the tessellations made by classmates.

Use prompts like these to promote class discussion:

- How many different two-block combinations did you find?

- Did all of the two-block combinations tessellate? If not, which did not? Why do you think these combinations did not tessellate?

- How do you know that you found all the possible combinations?

- How did you decide which way to put your shapes together? Was there more than one possible way?

- Did you try to make a special design with a combination of shapes that you were able to tessellate?

- Did you make any tessellations that contain symmetrical designs? Explain.

Extending the Activity

1. Have children select two different Pattern Blocks and make as many different tessellating designs as they can.
2. Have children repeat the activity using combinations of three different Pattern Blocks.

Where's the Mathematics?

In working through this activity, children find themselves confronted with two tasks—identifying all possible combinations of two different Pattern Blocks and testing the combinations to see whether they tessellate. Some children may approach these tasks simultaneously, randomly selecting the two types of blocks, attempting to tessellate them, and keeping track of the results. Other children may decide to first figure out what all the possible two-block combinations are. One way they might do this is to begin with one kind of block and pair it with the others. They might then take the other blocks and pair them with the remaining blocks, making sure that identical pairs such as red-blue and blue-red are not both counted. This table summarizes the results of this process, showing the 15 different two-block combinations:

Two-Block Combinations

yellow-red	red-blue	blue-green	green-orange	orange-tan
yellow-blue	red-green	blue-orange	green-tan	
yellow-green	red-orange	blue-tan		
yellow-orange	red-tan			
yellow-tan				

Children will use different methods to test the combinations to see if they tessellate. Although some children may be content to simply fit the blocks together indiscriminately, focusing on covering the paper with no gaps, others may try to create designs that show some kind of repeating pattern

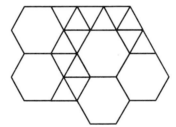 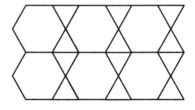

Some children may begin by making rows of blocks, leading to two-block tessellations containing striped designs in which each stripe is formed from one kind of block.

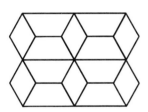

Orange–tan

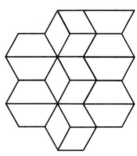

Blue–tan

Red–orange

Children come to realize that there may be more than one way for a two-block combination to tessellate. For example, here are three of the ways that the combination of red and blue blocks tessellate:

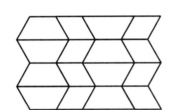
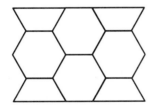

Children may also notice that some tessellations form patterns or designs that contain symmetry. For example, the tessellation shown below has 180° rotational symmetry as well as horizontal and vertical line symmetry.

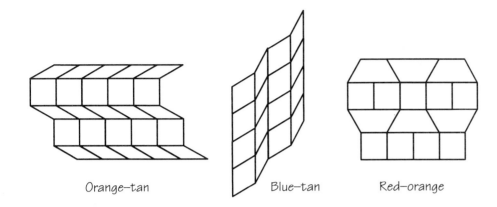

As they experiment with different combinations of blocks, children recognize that shapes that tessellate fit together in a particular way. Their observations may help them to understand why the yellow-tan and yellow-orange combinations do not tessellate. Children may explain that these shapes don't tessellate because their corners (angles) do not fit together in the way that the corners (angles) of shapes that tessellate do. Recognition of this relationship provides children with a glimpse of the mathematics involved in tessellations, allowing them to see tessellations as more than simply interesting designs.

TRAPEZOIDS 1–16

- **Properties of geometric figures**
- **Spatial visualization**
- **Congruence**
- **Equivalence**

Getting Ready

What You'll Need

Pattern Blocks, about 100 per group

Pattern Block triangle paper, page 90

Overhead Pattern Blocks (optional)

Overview

Children build trapezoids using specified numbers of Pattern Blocks. In this activity, children have the opportunity to:

- learn about the properties of trapezoids
- discover and use relationships among various geometric shapes
- develop spatial visualization skills

The Activity

You may want to review the meaning of parallel sides.

Introducing

- Display a trapezoid like the one shown. Have children count to determine that it is made of 16 Pattern Blocks.

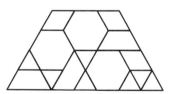

- Invite children to hold up the single Pattern Block that they think resembles this 16-block shape. Ask them to explain the resemblance they see.

- Identify both shapes as trapezoids. Then discuss with children what all trapezoids have in common. Establish that trapezoids are four-sided figures with exactly two sides that are parallel.

On Their Own

> **Can you make a trapezoid with any number of Pattern Blocks from 1 to 16?**
>
> - Work with your group to build trapezoids with different numbers of blocks.
>
> - Find a way to share the task so that your group can be sure of finding at least one trapezoid made with each number of blocks from 1 to 16.
>
> - Use Pattern Block triangle paper to record your arrangements.
>
> - Be prepared to talk about the strategies you used to find your solutions.

The Bigger Picture

Thinking and Sharing

Invite children to post their solutions. Arrange the solutions so that children can see some of the different trapezoid shapes for each number of Pattern Blocks.

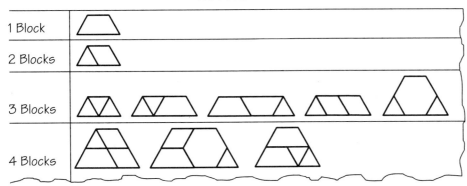

TRAPEZOIDS

Use prompts such as these to promote class discussion:

- Was it possible to make trapezoids using every number of blocks from 1 to 16?

- Were you able to use each of the six Pattern Block shapes in your trapezoids? Explain why or why not.

- Did you have a strategy for building trapezoids with different numbers of blocks? Explain how you worked.

- Did you notice any congruent pairs of trapezoids made from different numbers of blocks? How can you explain this?

- Do you think there may be other solutions that you haven't found yet? Give reasons for your thinking.

You may want to review the meaning of congruent.

Writing

Have children explain why some Pattern Blocks can be used to build trapezoids and some can't.

Where's the Mathematics?

This activity gives children an opportunity to explore many of the relationships that exist among the different Pattern Block shapes. As children work with the blocks, trying to build trapezoids, they discover that most of the blocks have sides of equal lengths and angles that allow them to fit together easily without leaving gaps. They may also discover that neither the orange square nor the tan rhombus can be used to make a trapezoid, since their angles are not compatible with the angles of the other blocks.

At least one trapezoid can be made with each number of Pattern Blocks from 1 to 16. Some children may discover that trapezoids can be built with different numbers of blocks just by extending each trapezoid lengthwise. For example, trapezoids can be built with every number of blocks from 2 to 16 using only blue parallelograms and one green triangle, as shown.

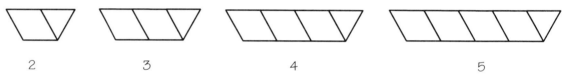

          2   3   4   5

Other children may use the strategy of adding rows of blocks to make trapezoids. They may also recognize patterns that may help them predict the number of blocks that could be used to form larger trapezoids. For example, the numbers of blocks used to build the trapezoids below form a pattern where the numbers differ by consecutive whole numbers.

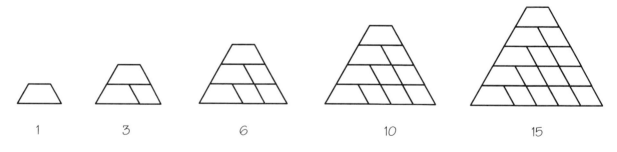

    1   3   6   10   15

Children may realize that they can find other solutions using this same kind of pattern but starting with a trapezoid containing a different number of blocks. This was done to produce the set of trapezoids shown on the next page. Here the first trapezoid contains two blocks instead of one.

Extending the Activity

1. Have children explore building triangles or parallelograms using from 1 to 16 Pattern Blocks in as many ways as possible.

2. Challenge children to find all the possible ways to build a trapezoid of a particular size. Ask, "What is the least number of blocks that can be used? What is the greatest number?"

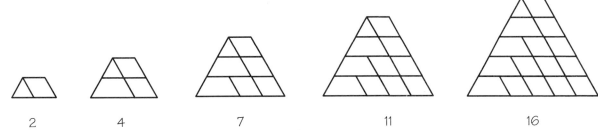

| 2 | 4 | 7 | 11 | 16 |

Some children may begin by making large trapezoids, such as the one in the *Introducing* section, and use equivalences to make substitutions producing congruent trapezoids made from different numbers of Pattern Blocks. For example, replacing two of the green triangles in the lower right-hand corner of trapezoid A below with a blue parallelogram produces trapezoid B made from 15 blocks.

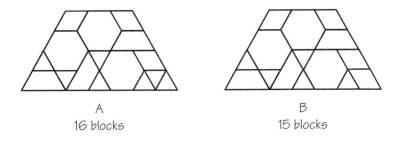

| A | B |
| 16 blocks | 15 blocks |

Similarly, replacing larger blocks with equivalent combinations of smaller blocks produces congruent trapezoids made from a greater number of blocks. In the trapezoids below, the red trapezoids in the lower left- and right-hand corners of trapezoid C have each been replaced with a blue parallelogram and a green triangle, producing trapezoid D made from 13 blocks.

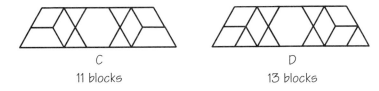

| C | D |
| 11 blocks | 13 blocks |

In sharing their solutions, children discover the variety of different-shaped trapezoids that can be made using Pattern Blocks. They also can see that congruent trapezoids may be made from different numbers and arrangements of blocks.

WHAT'S MY SHAPE WORTH?

Getting Ready

What You'll Need

Pattern Blocks (no orange or tan), about 100 per group

Crayons

Overhead Pattern Blocks (optional)

Overview

Children create Pattern Block designs and determine the "monetary value" of their designs based on a value assigned to one of the shapes. In this activity, children have the opportunity to:

◆ investigate relationships among the areas of different shapes

◆ perform computations with money

◆ discover that shapes with the same area may look different

The Activity

Introducing

◆ Display this Pattern Block design.

◆ Ask children to imagine that this design costs a certain amount of money and that the green triangle is worth 2¢.

◆ Have children work with a partner to figure out what the complete design costs. Tell them to be ready to explain how they arrived at their answer.

◆ Invite volunteers to share their solutions and their thinking.

On Their Own

If Pattern Block shapes had a money value, how could you use the value of 1 block to figure out the cost of a design that uses 4 different kinds of blocks?

- Make a design using 10 Pattern Blocks. Use any combination of green, blue, red, or yellow blocks. Your design must have at least one of each kind of block.

- Find the total cost of your design if the blue parallelogram is worth 10¢.

- Record your design by tracing it onto paper and coloring it.

- Write the cost of your design on the back of the paper.

- Exchange pictures with other members of your group and find the cost of each person's design.

- Check your solutions by looking on the back of each design.

- Put your group's designs in order from least expensive to most expensive.

The Bigger Picture

Thinking and Sharing

Invite children to discuss their methods for finding the total cost of various designs. Then have the class post their designs in order from least expensive to most expensive.

Use prompts like these to promote class discussion:

- What was your strategy for finding the total cost of a design? Did anyone use a different strategy? What was it?

- What do you notice about designs that have the same cost?

- What can you discover when you see all the designs arranged in order from the least expensive to the most expensive?

- Why do you think the directions excluded the use of the orange and tan blocks?

Writing

Have children write a set of directions for finding the cost of any design.

Extending the Activity

1. Have children repeat the activity, assigning the yellow hexagon a value of 36¢.

2. Have children assign a certain value to the blue parallelogram and find the cost of the most expensive and least expensive designs they can build using 10 blocks. As in the activity, children's designs must have at least one green, one blue, one red, and one yellow block.

Where's the Mathematics?

By starting with an assigned value for one Pattern Block and using that value to find the value of the other blocks, children use proportional reasoning based on their understanding of the relative sizes of the blocks. If they know—or discover through this activity—that all of the blocks can be built from green triangles, their strategy for finding the values of the Pattern Blocks may be as follows: Since the green triangle is half the size of the blue parallelogram, its value is half the value of the parallelogram, or 5¢. Since the red trapezoid is three times the size of the green triangle, its value is three times that of the green triangle, or 15¢. Likewise, the value of the yellow hexagon is six times the value of the green triangle, or 30¢. Since the green triangle does not easily compare in size to the orange square or the tan rhombus, it would be hard to figure out their values, and so it is a good idea to not use them in the designs.

Once children have determined the value of each block, there are a number of ways in which they may find the cost of a design. It is important for children to understand that there are many ways to discover the total value of their design, and they should use a way that makes sense to them. For example, for the design below, some children may simply add the values of each of the ten blocks: 30¢ + 30¢ + 30¢ + 15¢ + 15¢ + 10¢ + 10¢ + 10¢ + 5¢ + 5¢ = 160¢, or $1.60.

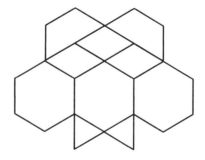

Other children may collect like blocks and multiply the value of each block by the number of blocks in the collection. They can then add the products

3. Ask children to again assume that a blue parallelogram is worth 10¢ and to build a design that costs exactly $1.00. They may use any combination of red, blue, yellow, and green blocks, at least one of each kind of block. Have children share their designs and discuss the variety of designs that are possible.

---

to determine the total cost. Their work for the preceding design might look like this:

$$3 \times 30¢ = 90¢$$
$$2 \times 15¢ = 30¢$$
$$3 \times 10¢ = 30¢$$
$$2 \times 5¢ = 10¢$$

total: 160¢, or $1.60

Since each design must contain at least one of each kind of block, the least expensive design contains seven triangles, one parallelogram, one trapezoid, and one hexagon and costs $0.90. The most expensive design contains seven hexagons, one trapezoid, one parallelogram, and one triangle and costs $2.40. As children organize their designs from least expensive to most expensive, they may make several observations. Some children may notice that the cost of any design is a multiple of 5. This is because every design can be made from green triangles, and the value of the green triangle is 5¢. Another observation children may make is that the larger the shape, the costlier the shape. Still another is that designs using different combinations of blocks may cost the same. Children who recognize this last relationship may be able to make the connection between the area of a design and the cost, realizing that designs that cost the same do so because they have the same area. For example, designs A and B below are made from different combinations of blocks, yet each has an area equivalent to 24 green triangles and costs $1.20. This observation may also help children to understand how shapes that look quite different may have the same area.

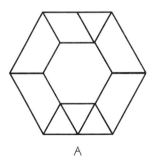

A

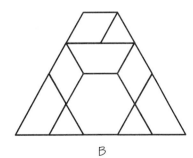

B

WHAT'S NEXT?

- **Looking for patterns**
- **Predicting**

Getting Ready

What You'll Need

Pattern Blocks, about 50 per pair

Paper strips (2 in. by 16 in.), 1 per pair

Hundreds charts, 1 per pair

Crayons

Overhead Pattern Blocks (optional)

Overview

Children create, record, and predict repeating patterns using Pattern Blocks. They then relate their patterns to number patterns by using a hundreds chart. In this activity, children have the opportunity to:

- ◆ discover that patterns are predictable
- ◆ connect visual patterns to numerical patterns
- ◆ recognize that there are multiple ways to solve a problem

The Activity

The blocks may also be placed in a line like this:

Introducing

- ◆ Ask children to describe what a pattern is.
- ◆ Show children this arrangement of blocks and explain that it shows a repeating pattern.

- ◆ Invite volunteers to tell which blocks they think would come next.
- ◆ Ask children to continue the pattern until the 15th block.
- ◆ Once children have firmly established the pattern, ask them to figure out what the 23rd block will be. Have them share their reasoning.
- ◆ Show children how to record the repeating pattern on a hundreds chart by coloring. Do not complete the hundreds chart.
- ◆ Ask children to share any patterns they notice and to use them to predict what color the 50th block will be.

On Their Own

Can you use Pattern Blocks to create a pattern showing a repeating design?

- Working with a partner, choose several different kinds of Pattern Blocks and make a pattern that shows a design that repeats by the 5th block or sooner. Some examples are shown below.

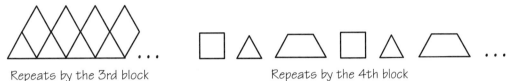

Repeats by the 3rd block   Repeats by the 4th block

- Record the first 12 blocks of your pattern by tracing and coloring them on a paper strip.

- Predict what the 20th block will be.

- Now color the squares on a hundreds chart to match the colors in your pattern. Color only up to square 20 on the chart. See if it matches your prediction for the 20th block.

- Use your hundreds chart to predict what the 89th block will be. Record your prediction.

- Now check your prediction by coloring all the squares in your chart through the 89th square.

- Look for patterns in your chart that could help you to predict the color of any numbered square on your hundreds chart.

The Bigger Picture

Thinking and Sharing

Display the pattern strips made by each pair. Invite children to compare the patterns on the strips and to talk about what they notice.

Use prompts like these to promote class discussion:

- What is the basic repeating pattern in each pattern? How do you know?

- Which patterns are similar even though they use different blocks?

- Look at this pattern. What color do you think the 25th block will be? How did you figure it out?

Then have children display their hundreds charts next to their pattern strips.

- What patterns do you notice on the hundreds charts?

- How are the patterns in the hundreds chart related to the patterns on the pattern strips?

Writing

Write a set of directions explaining how to use your pattern to figure out the color of any number on the hundreds chart.

Where's the Mathematics?

Through creating their own patterns and studying the patterns created by others, children may come to realize that patterns must repeat in a predictable way and that the colors as well as the sequence of blocks are important. For example, some children may feel that the pattern below repeats since the blue block appears every four blocks—in the first, fifth, and ninth positions—and the trios of in-between blocks are always the same color.

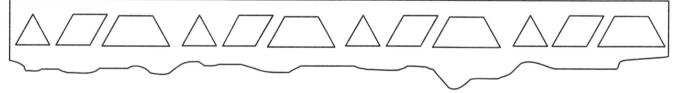

Children should come to realize this kind of pattern is not (yet) predictable since it is impossible to say for certain what the color of the next in-between trio will be. As children share patterns it should become apparent that if someone else cannot figure out what the next blocks in their pattern will be, the pattern may not be predictable.

Many children may make patterns that can be easily identified, such as the one below. Looking at the strip with the traced Pattern Blocks, children may identify the 20th block as blue by sketching or visualizing the next eight blocks.

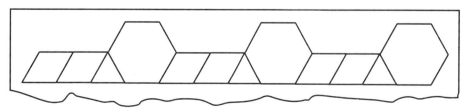

Some children may be able to look at the strip, notice that the repeating part or period consists of three blocks, and see a pattern of counting by threes. Using this pattern they can determine that the green triangles are in positions 1, 4, 7, 10, 13, 16, 19, 22, 25.... Likewise, the blue parallelograms are in positions 2, 5, 8, 11, 14, 17, 20, 23..., and the red trapezoids are in positions 3, 6, 9, 12, 15, 18, 21, 24....

For patterns that repeat every four blocks, children may use repeated addition by four to find the colors of particular blocks. For example, in the pattern shown here, the blue parallelograms are in positions 1, 5,

Extending the Activity

1. Have children repeat the activity with a pattern that repeats by the eighth block.

2. Have children sort the hundreds charts in several different ways and explain the categories they used.

3. Have children repeat the activity with a growth pattern such as red, green; red, green, green; red, green, green, green, and so on.

9, 13, 17, 21, 25..., and 2, 6, 10, 14, 18, 22, 26.... The green triangles are in positions 3, 7, 11, 15, 19, 23, 27..., and the yellow hexagons are in positions 4, 8, 12, 16, 20, 24, 28....

By relating repeating patterns to the hundreds chart, children can see numerical patterns and their connections to the color patterns. With the pattern green-blue-red, children may see that the pattern has a period of three blocks and that all multiples of 3 will be colored red. From this information, children might be able to predict that 39 will be red. They may also be able to reason that 40 will be green because green is always one after red (39). Some children may even use division. For example, to find out what the color of a particular block would be, they might divide the position number of the block by the period, which is 3 in this pattern, and look at the remainder. If the remainder is 1, the block is green; if the remainder is 2, the block is blue; and if there is no remainder, the block is red. Similar methods can be used when working with patterns having different length periods.

Some children may fill the chart one number at a time until they reach 100. Others may see vertical, horizontal, or diagonal patterns emerging after coloring in only a few rows. These patterns may help them to quickly and accurately complete their charts. For example, after filling in a few rows of this chart for the green-blue-red pattern, children may see how the numbers with the same color occur diagonally. This knowledge can help them to complete the chart without counting by threes.

For patterns with longer periods, or periods that contain repeating colors, children may need to fill in more rows of the hundreds chart before they see patterns. The chart shown here for a blue-blue-green-yellow pattern shows blue spaces in pairs forming "steps" that descend from left to right: 1-2, 13-14, 25-26, 37-38, 49-50.... Another pattern shows the green spaces in every other row of the odd-numbered columns and the yellow spaces in every other row of the even-numbered columns.

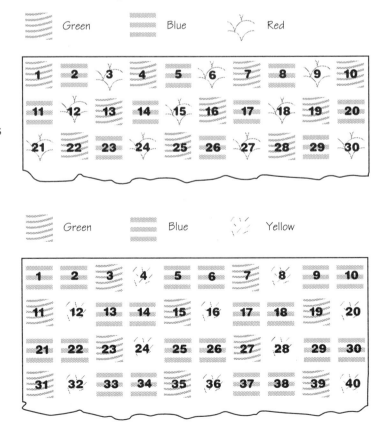

WHAT'S THE PERIMETER?

- Perimeter
- Comparing geometric shapes

Getting Ready

What You'll Need

Pattern Blocks, 6 each of red, green, yellow, and blue per pair

Pattern Block triangle paper, page 90

Scissors

Overhead Pattern Blocks (optional)

Overview

Children investigate the different perimeters of shapes that can be made using one set of six Pattern Blocks. In this activity, children have the opportunity to:

- ◆ determine the perimeters of various shapes
- ◆ build a variety of configurations using the same six shapes
- ◆ generalize about geometric shapes and their perimeters

The Activity

Introducing

- ◆ Review the concept of *perimeter* as the distance around a shape.
- ◆ Establish the length of one side of the green Pattern Block as one unit of perimeter.
- ◆ Have children compare the length of a side of the green triangle to the length of the sides of each of the other Pattern Blocks. Ask them to find the perimeter of each block.

   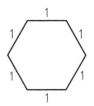

- ◆ Now have children put two green triangles together so that they share a common side. Ask them to determine the perimeter of this new shape.
- ◆ Invite volunteers to share their results.

On Their Own

What are all the possible perimeters of shapes that can be made using a set of 6 Pattern Blocks?

- Working with a partner, choose a variety of 6 blocks. Place them together to form a shape so that each block shares at least 1 full unit of length with another block. A full unit of length is equal to a side of a green triangle.

- Make sure that the blocks in your shape do not surround any empty spaces.

- Color your shape on triangle paper. Then figure out and record its perimeter.

- Rearrange the same 6 blocks and repeat the process until you think you have found all the possible perimeters of shapes that can be made using these 6 blocks.

- Cut out all your shapes.

- Be ready to talk about your shapes and their perimeters.

The Bigger Picture

Thinking and Sharing

Ask one pair of partners to display their recordings and tell the perimeter of each of the shapes they made with their collection of blocks. If any other pairs used the same set of blocks, have them display their recordings also. If groups who have worked with the same blocks don't agree on what perimeters can be obtained, invite the entire class to work with those blocks to reach agreement. Post these shapes by perimeter from smallest to largest. Repeat this process until all pairs have posted and ordered their shapes.

Use prompts like these to promote class discussion:

- Did you get the same perimeter in more than one way with your blocks? Why is this possible?

- What are all the possible perimeters of shapes that can be made using your set of blocks? Do all sets of blocks have the same range of perimeters?

- Did some groups get the same perimeters using different blocks? How can you explain this?

- How would you describe the arrangements of blocks that have the smallest perimeter? the largest perimeter?

- How do the arrangements with the smallest perimeters differ from those with the largest perimeters?

- Why are fewer perimeters possible with some blocks than with others?

Extending the Activity

Give children a larger number of blocks, such as two yellow hexagons, three red trapezoids, three blue parallelograms, and two green triangles. Have children find and record all the different perimeters of shapes they can make and arrange them from smallest to largest. Ask children to explain how their earlier exploration helped them to make predictions about perimeters of shapes that could be made using these blocks.

Where's the Mathematics?

As they explore with their Pattern Blocks and share their results with other groups, children come to realize that it is possible to make shapes having the same perimeter using different arrangements of the same blocks.

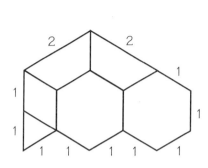

Perimeter = 13 units

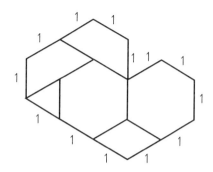

Perimeter = 13 units

Children also discover that the same perimeters can be obtained using different sets of blocks.

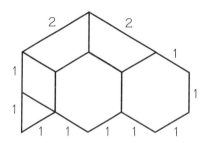

Perimeter = 13 units

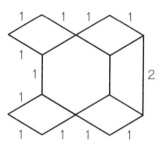

Perimeter = 13 units

Examining their recordings, children can observe that the more closely they fit their blocks together—that is, the more sides the shapes share—the smaller the perimeter of their shape will be. Conversely, the more they stretch out their shapes, the greater the perimeter will be.

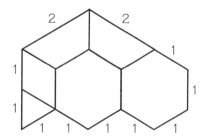

Perimeter = 13 units

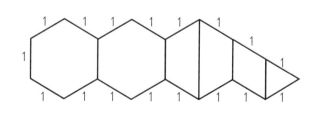

Perimeter = 17 units

With some sets of six blocks, three or four different perimeters will be possible. With other sets, (for example, four green triangles and two blue parallelograms) only two different perimeters will be possible. Children may realize that the range of perimeters will vary, depending upon the blocks chosen and how these blocks can be fitted together.

Children may also discover that any set of blocks whose perimeters total an odd number will form shapes having only odd-numbered perimeters, and any set whose perimeters total an even number will form shapes having only even-numbered perimeters. They may also notice that it is possible to make shapes having perimeters of each of the odd (or even) numbers between the smallest and greatest perimeters they find. For example, the six blocks shown below have a total perimeter of 25 units and can be used to form shapes having perimeters 11 units, 13 units, and 15 units, respectively.

Total perimeter = 25 units

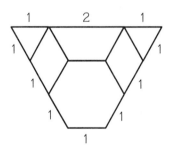

Perimeter = 11 units

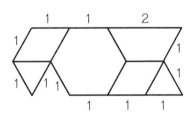

Perimeter = 13 units

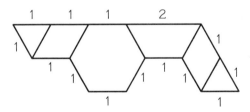

Perimeter = 15 units

WIPE OUT!

Getting Ready

What You'll Need

Pattern Blocks, about 30 per pair

Number cubes with sides labeled
1/2, 1/3, 1/3, 1/6, 1/6, and 1/6,
1 per pair

Overhead Pattern Blocks (optional)

Overview

In this game for two players, children use Pattern Blocks to represent fractional parts of the yellow hexagon. In this activity, children have the opportunity to:

◆ work with equivalent fractions

◆ develop problem-solving strategies within the context of a game

◆ consider the role of probability in a game that involves both skill and chance

The Activity

Sometimes children get impatient to roll the cube before their partner has had a chance to decide what to do. You may want to have children hold on to the cube until they have completed their turn. This will keep the pace sensible and fair.

Introducing

◆ Tell children that they are going to play a game called *Wipe Out!*, which involves Pattern Block pieces and a cube marked with fractions.

◆ Hold up one of the fraction cubes and turn it as you ask children to call out the fractions they see on each face.

◆ Go over the game rules given in *On Their Own*.

◆ Now model the game for children. It may be helpful to talk about your choices each time you roll the cube. For example, on the first roll you could discuss some of the different combinations of blocks you might choose in exchanging your yellow hexagon.

On Their Own

Play *Wipe Out!*

Here are the rules:

1. This is a game for 2 players. The object is to be the first player to get rid of his or her blocks.

2. Each player begins with a yellow hexagon. This piece is considered 1.

3. Players take turns rolling a fraction cube with faces labeled ½, ⅓, or ⅙. These fractions represent parts of the hexagon.

4. After rolling the cube, a player can make 1 of 3 choices:

   - A player can exchange blocks for other blocks that have the same value. (For example, if a player rolls ½, but has only a yellow hexagon, that player can return the yellow hexagon to the pile, take a red trapezoid and 3 green triangles instead, and hope that the roll on the next turn will be a ½ or ⅙).

   - A player can get rid of a block. This is possible only if:

     (1) the player has already traded the hexagon for blocks of the same value AND

     (2) the player has a block that represents the same fractional part of a hexagon as that shown on the top face of the cube. (For example, if the cube shows ½, the player can only get rid of a red trapezoid.)

   - A player can skip a turn.

5. The first player to get rid of his or her blocks wins the game.

- Play the game several times to see if you can come up with a good strategy for wiping out your hexagon as quickly as possible.

The Bigger Picture

Thinking and Sharing

Invite children to talk about their games and describe some of the thinking they did.

Use prompts like these to promote class discussion:

- What did you notice as you played *Wipe Out!?*
- Is it ever a good idea to skip your turn? Why or why not?
- When did you find it advantageous to exchange blocks? Why?
- Did the labeling on the number cube affect your choice of blocks? If so, how?
- What have you noticed about the probability of rolling ½, ⅓, or ⅙?
- What winning strategies did you discover?
- What is the least number of rolls with which it is possible to win? What is the greatest number? Explain.

Writing

Have children pretend to write to someone who has never played the game *Wipe Out!* before. Tell them to describe a successful strategy that they discovered.

Extending the Activity

1. Have children play the game with this change in the rules: Players may get rid of blocks that are equivalent to the fraction they roll. For example,

Where's the Mathematics?

While playing *Wipe Out!* children visualize and gain an understanding of fractional relationships. They identify the red trapezoid as 1/2, the blue parallelogram as 1/3, and the green triangle as 1/6. When they exercise the option of exchanging blocks, they have a chance to informally, yet concretely, explore fraction equivalency. For example, if they exchange a blue parallelogram for two green triangles, they are learning that 1/3 = 1/6 + 1/6 or 1/3 = 2/6. If they exchange a red trapezoid for a blue parallelogram and a green triangle, they learn that 1/2 = 1/3 + 1/6. If they exchange the yellow hexagon for a red trapezoid, a blue parallelogram, and a green triangle, they learn that 1 = 1/2 + 1/3 + 1/6.

Children who do not immediately focus on the relative probabilities of rolling 1/2, 1/3, and 1/6 may decide on their first turn to make the choice of exchanging the yellow hexagon for one red trapezoid, one blue parallelogram, and one green triangle. With this strategy, they guarantee that on their second turn they will be able to remove a block. If they roll a 1/6 on the second turn they can remove a green triangle and will be left with a red trapezoid and a blue parallelogram.

First roll   Second roll

if they roll 1/2, they may remove a red trapezoid, a blue parallelogram and a green triangle, or three green triangles.

2. Have children play the game with two or three yellow hexagons.

3. Have children explore probability as they play *Wipe Out!* Direct them to make a chart with the headings 1/2, 1/3, and 1/6. Ask children to roll the fraction cube and use tally marks to record how often each fraction is rolled during the game. Encourage children to find out how their data changes as they go from 10 rolls to 20, 30, or more.

If they roll a 1/6 on the third turn, they may choose to skip a turn because they feel that 1/2 and 1/3 are "due" as rolls. If they continue to roll 1/6, they may eventually consider using a turn to exchange the red trapezoid or the blue parallelogram for some green triangles.

The scenario for the shortest game—three rolls—would be this: On the first roll, the yellow hexagon is exchanged for two red trapezoids; 1/2 is rolled on each of the next two turns and a red trapezoid is removed each time. There is no scenario for the longest game, since a game could go on almost indefinitely if a player continues to be unlucky on his or her rolls or makes exchanges that don't pan out.

After playing the game several times, children begin to notice that some fractions occur more frequently than others. They may be able to relate this to the faces of the cube: There are three out of six chances of rolling 1/6, two out of six chances of rolling 1/3, and one out of six chances of rolling 1/2. If children are aware of these probabilities, they are likely to use them to make decisions about exchanging blocks or taking chances on the blocks they already have. For example, a player who has just started the game may decide to exchange the yellow hexagon for six triangles because the probability of getting 1/6 is the greatest. The player may then decide not to exchange again, waiting to roll 1/6s and removing one green triangle at a time. Another player who recognizes that 1/6 will not necessarily come up half the time may exchange the hexagon for a variety of blocks so that all bases are covered and then exchange for smaller blocks so that different choices are available as the game progresses.

PATTERN BLOCK SHAPES

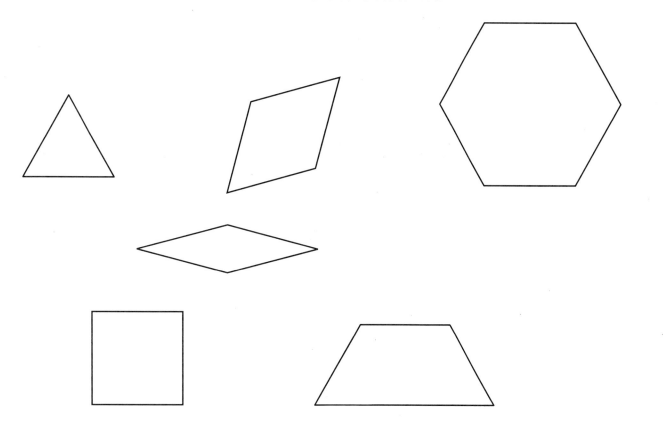

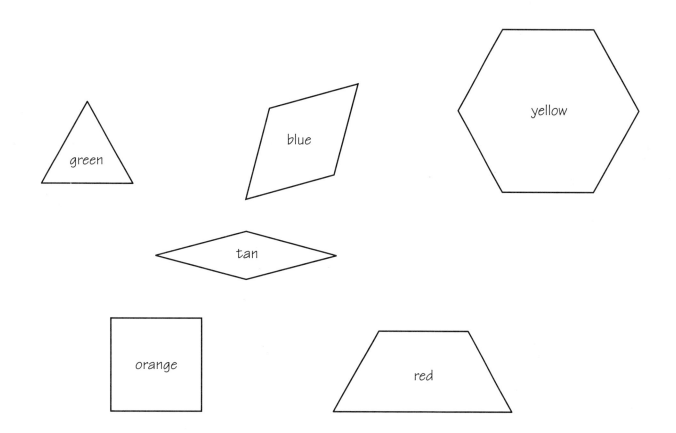

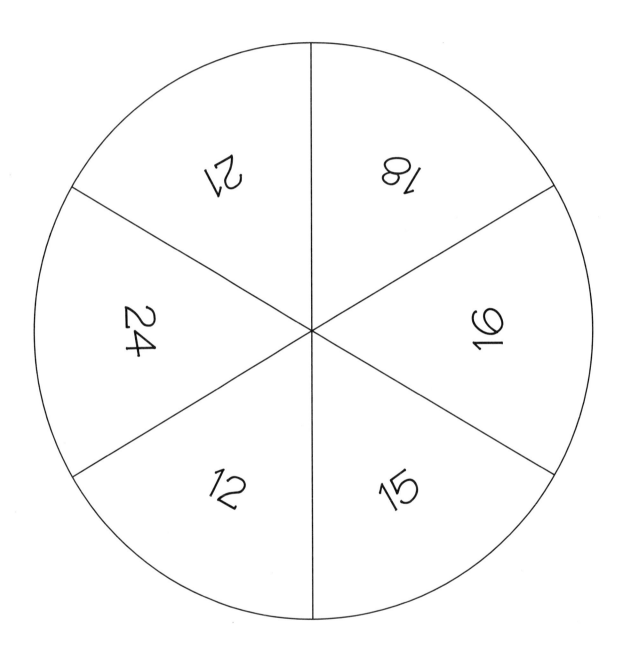

THE LAST BLOCK
GAME BOARD

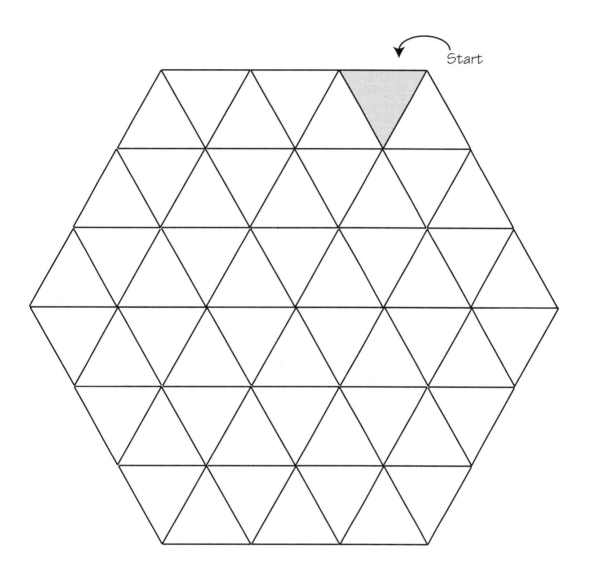

Start

PATTERN BLOCK WRITING PAPER

_____

_____

_____

_____

_____

_____